"Life and LOVE do NOT get easier as we ___
Marriage: Staying in Love as Your Odomete ___
have packed up golden nuggets of affection, wisdom, and wit to bless and build us on this journey of loving each other well for the miles ahead. HOP IN! Enjoy the road trip of marriage. The REST of love can be the BEST of love!"

—**Pam Farrel**, co-author of bestselling *Men Are Like Waffles, Women Are Like Spaghetti* and *52 Ways to Wow Your Husband: Put a Smile on His Face*

"Nothing like a chuckle to lighten up a heavy topic. In *Classic Marriage*, Michelle and Phil are just the best down-to-earth encouragers, offering hope for a God-inspired marriage tune-up."

—**Rhonda Rhea**, TV personality, humor columnist, and author of 18 books, including the award-winning rom-coms, *Turtles in the Road* and *Off-Script & Over-Caffeinated*

"This is a GREAT read. It's fun, practical and there are gems of wisdom on every page. I loved the interaction on the pages with Michelle and Phil. Your marriage can be refreshed and strengthened with this very enjoyable book."

—**Jim Burns, PhD,** President, HomeWord, author of *Doing Life With Your Adult Children: Keep Your Mouth Shut and the Welcome Mat Out*

"Michelle Rayburn's new book, *Classic Marriage: Staying in Love as Your Odometer Climbs* is a great read for couples seeking to tune up the clunker and turn it into a classic. The reader is treated to a two-for-one dose of insightful experience and candid stories from their 30+ year marriage. Michelle does the heavy lifting of authoring, sharing personal moments and life lessons, both the magic and the nearly tragic. Hubby Phil pops in briefly along the way bringing his own brand of support. He is dry, funny, and occasionally snarky. Their suggestions for enriching your relationship are practical and simple and stimulate new ways to deal with old issues. This is a lighthearted book with a serious message. Don't miss it."

—**Deb DeArmond**, writing coach, speaker, and award-winning author of books on family and marriage including: *Don't Go to Bed Angry. Stay Up and Fight!* and *I Choose You Today*

"It is a rare author who can dispense practical wisdom, season it with humor and keep you turning the pages. Michelle Rayburn is one of those people. If you can read this book without smiling, you might want to check your pulse. Applying the guidelines she offers can move your marriage on the front burner. As a husband of 52 years I found her book delightful and extremely helpful."

—**Ken Davis**, speaker, comedian, communication coach, 52-year marriage survivor

"In *Classic Marriage*, the Rayburns have taken a serious topic and made it fun with laugh-out-loud humor and relatable stories. With an emphasis on preventive maintenance, this is a go-to resource for couples who want to enrich their relationship and achieve a loving, joyful marriage."

—**Shel Harrington**, Family Law Attorney, Speaker and blogger at **shelharrington.com**

"Michelle and Phil not only share their insight as to how to accept each other's differences, they do so with humor and communication tools that will help any couple—regardless of how long they've been married—to stay their course and avoid wrong turns that often lead to separation or divorce."

—**Joe and Michelle Williams**, authors of *Yes, Your Marriage Can Be Saved* (Focus on the Family/Tyndale House, 2007) and Founders of Marriage 911 God's Way
www.Marriage911Godsway.com

"*Classic Marriage* is a fabulous resource! This book would be perfect for couples to read together as it gives dual perspectives and insights from the author and her husband. In addition, it contains quality questions to help couples dive deeper in their marriage. Whether your relationships needs a maintenance check, tune-up, or complete overhaul, grab a copy of *Classic Marriage* and hold on for the ride!"

—**Clint and Penny A. Bragg**, authors of *Your Marriage, God's Mission*
www.InverseMinistries.org

"Whether you have been married for a long time or only a few years, this book is chock-full of practical tools to help you get under the hood and work on your relationship. With humor, biblical insights, and honest stories about their struggles and victories, Michelle and Phil prove that marriage isn't a fairy tale... but it can be fun and joy-filled."

—**Carey and Dena Dyer**, co-authors of *Love at First Fight: 52 Story-Based Meditations for Married Couples* (Barbour, 2016)

"Why settle for 'just' married when you can choose to pursue the best marriage you can possibly have?" If you agree with this question, then you will love this book! It is all about helping you to make your relationship soar. Through a gentle approach using humor and a conversational writing style, Michelle weaves a very practical guide to marriage. What makes the book so real for the husbands are the comments made by Phil. I highly recommend this book for married couples who want to have fun along the way to the best marriage possible."

—**Dave Howe**, Live Pure Ministries, author of *Live Pure and Free: The 90-Day Game Changer*, winner of The Christian Indy Award for 2019

"A funny, frank, and wise look at building a marriage. In *Classic Marriage*, high school sweethearts and now empty nesters Michelle and Phil Rayburn offer a practical blueprint for inhabiting our own 'I do.' Packed with tools to help a relationship thrive through the decades."

—**Jane Rubietta**, international speaker and author of *Radiance: Finding Light in Dark Places* and *Worry Less, Live More*

"Like friends who are a little further down the marriage road, Michelle and Phil offer come-alongside advice without condemning. With candid examples of how God has changed them and is still working on their marriage, they provide practical and biblical tools for other couples."

—**Ginger Kolbaba** is a bestselling, award-winning author, speaker, and editor

"*Classic Marriage* is a practical book on having the kind of marriage that will thrive. It combines humor, Phil's comments (you're going to love Phil) and practical advice from a marriage that has stood the test of time. I would buy this book, and I highly recommend it to you!"

—**Rev. Greg Speck**, youth and family communicator who speaks for the Weekend to Remember marriage conferences, author of four books

"This is a wonderfully helpful, fun resource for couples, whether you've been married for five months or five decades. Written with humor and wisdom, Biblical insight and real-world experience, Michelle Rayburn delivers a book that we married couples need. Every marriage needs constant attention, maintenance, and care, and *Classic Marriage* might just be what you and your spouse need. Buy this book, buy it for a couple you know and dig in!"

—**Daniel Darling**, pastor and best-selling author of several books including, *The Dignity Revolution*, *The Characters of Christmas*, and *A Way With Words*

"Michelle and Phil Rayburn would be a fun couple to take with you and your spouse on a road trip! Michelle's wise and witty writing and Phil's snarky asides make this marriage book an enjoyable and entertaining ride. Grab some snacks and hop in!"

—**James N. Watkins**, award-winning author and husband of 46 years

"Two words I would use to describe *Classic Marriage*. Real and relevant. Two attributes that are much needed in our day and age. Michelle and Phil give real world wisdom on how to keep a marriage strong through each season of life, using a healthy dose of transparency and humor."

—**Darren Cox**, Christian counselor, founder of Anchor Bay Counseling
anchorbaycounseling.com

"Michelle has given couples a fun, vibrant, humorous, and poignant look at the journey of marriage over time. She provides the help and instructions to the reader, while her husband offers the husband insights (in true husband form) in a short, matter-of-fact style that allows husbands the ability to identify with the other half of their 'Usness.' From romance to maturity in love over time, they provide helpful tips and principles for any couple to make a difference that leads to a more loving and mature relationship. I believe you will find this work of theirs not just easy to read, but with their helpful tools, easy to implement. I found myself actually picturing myself in the room with them, listening to them talk to me."

—**Richard "Rick" Marks**, PhD, LPC, founder of RelateWell, LLC

"Just like a classic car, a 'classic marriage' benefits from tune-ups and TLC. Michelle Rayburn's book is written with humor and insight from a wife and husband's perspective, as Phil add his comments throughout the book. Everyday situations from different seasons of marriage are used to teach principles to help your marriage. Each chapter has well thought out discussion questions for couples to tune up their communication, strengthening their relationship."

—**Nancy Kay Grace**, speaker and author of *The Grace Impact*. Nancy has been a part of the international ministry of United Marriage Encounter for more than 25 years as a presenter or board member. **www.nancykaygrace.com**

"This book paints a real picture of marriages that last through the years . . . I particularly enjoyed her husband's comments. It was fun to see how a guy reacts to the way women write and describe their marriages. Their book makes a good book for a couple to read on dates nights."

—**Joyce Zook**, international speaker, certified Christian life and marriage coach, author of *12 Keys for Marriage Success – A Biblical Perspective for Wives*

"Michelle Rayburn has brought a fresh approach to helping couples understand each other. It was interesting, helpful, and sometimes humorous to see the difference in the way she reveals the communication differences between a husband and wife. This book will be helpful to marriages of many years. However, if you need a gift for newlyweds, this book would be a gift that would serve the couple throughout their marriage. I very much look forward to putting it on my list of books referred to my counselees!"

—**Nancy Anderson-Morris**, pastoral care counselor, advanced trauma resolution specialist

Classic Marriage

STAYING IN LOVE AS YOUR ODOMETER CLIMBS

Michelle Rayburn

with commentary by
PHIL RAYBURN

FAITH CREATIVITY
LIFE BOOKS

Proofreader: Nancy Graves
Cover, interior design, typesetting and eBook design: Michelle Rayburn
Cover images: Elizabeth "Izzy" Backus, Izzy B Photography

Printed in the United States of America
2020—First Edition

For our sons, Dallas and Austin
Please learn from our mistakes,
be brave enough to admit yours,
and be wise enough to correct them.

Table of Contents

Introduction

This is a book for couples. I (Michelle) have a sweet little picture in my mind of a husband and wife sitting together somewhere as they read the book and discuss the chapters. They talk about concepts and take turns acknowledging one another's feelings with kindness, sensitivity, and gentleness.

Wait! Don't leave!

I'm kidding. I live in the real world, and I know if this would not likely happen in our marriage, there is a pretty good chance that it won't happen in yours either. For one, I love to read, and Phil thinks books are evil. Well not evil, exactly. He loves the Bible. And he likes books, I think, but he didn't have a great experience with them in his formative years. So, I highly doubt we would be on the same page—pun intended—when it comes to reading together.

After observing other couples, I've discovered that many husbands don't love books. I know, this isn't always the case. But even the ones who love to read have diverse tastes from their sweethearts. Yet, I've noted that women love to pick up books at conferences and bookstores to bring them home hoping their husbands will eagerly devour the contents. With a warped vision of reality, they dream of paging through the chapters together as they happily apply the principles to their own marriage—as if their husbands are like the girls at book club.

That's a formula for conflict. Such an expectation is likely to have more of a harmful effect than a helpful one. And the books will be blamed. Oh, the poor books that sit on coffee tables and nightstands after a wife experiences discouraging results from trying to force feed information to her husband.

When an attempt to read together doesn't work out, she will read the book herself and feed him bites from her plate. She'll say things such as, "Honey, in the book, *Best Marriage on Earth*, Dr. Expert says we should be going on a date every week and discussing our relationship more."

She watches the flashy glow of the television on her husband's face as he gives her a tiny glance over his glasses. Believing she has his attention, she continues, "Dr. E's principles have changed my life. I think you should read this book."

Should. My husband doesn't love when that word comes from my lips, even when they're sporting poppy-pink lip gloss. Have you ever noticed how similar the word should is to the word shoulder? Add two more letters and should shows its true character as a weight piled onto the shoulders of the one who doesn't wish to be burdened.

We wrote this book for all of the wives who want their husbands to read a book on marriage but who don't think it's likely to happen. That's why Phil, who doesn't love books, helped me write this one. He worked through each chapter as we discussed our own journey. He provided both entertaining and wise insight about each topic. He also made some comments that will never in a million years make it to the printed page! Inappropriate much?

This project was a bit like going through our own self-guided marriage therapy to look back over thirty years—as our mileage climbed—to process our own learning moments.

Throughout each chapter you'll find summaries of the main ideas as well as witty comments—and possibly some sarcasm—all from Phil's perspective. At the end of each chapter, you'll find discussion questions to use together as a little tune-up for your relationship. We encourage you to make a habit of setting aside time each week to talk before the check engine light comes on.

If you can go out on a date, the questions can be used to start meaningful conversation over a meal or on a walk after dinner. Or if you choose to stay in, which is one of our favorite cheap dates, prepare a meal together and then have a heart-to-heart over dessert. The discussion questions will help you laugh, reminisce, restore, and take steps toward building a sense of unity and closeness. Some might spark conflict and provide an opportunity to practice handling it in a healthy way. You'll also find the Tune-Up Time discussion questions from the end of each chapter at **www.classicmarriagebook.com**. They are available in a printable or digital version to take with you on your date via paper or smartphone.

Husbands, you have permission to flip through the book and read Phil's comments scattered throughout each chapter while your wife takes her time with the longer content. Or vice versa, if you're both from an opposite universe where the husband loves to read and the wife prefers to get info from Instagram rather than ink on a page. Either way is okay.

Guys, if you do read only Phil's comments, you might be able to finish "reading" this book in an afternoon—long before your wife. And that would be a feather in your cap. You will be the one saying, "Dr. Expert says . . . " Except, there is no Dr. Expert here, just two everyday people who figured out marriage isn't always easy, and never perfect, but always worth the effort.

You see, Phil has spent years of our relationship with his head under the hood of a truck, a Jeep, or a broken minivan. I say years because, cumulatively, that's what it adds up to. An evening here or a Saturday there can add up to a lot of time when working on classic cars. He would much rather fix up an "old faithful" than purchase a new vehicle.

In fact, several years ago we purchased the first new car we have ever owned, mostly because I was tired of breaking down along the road and having my van hauled home on a flatbed trailer. Phil says this is all part of the adventure, and he prefers to still drive a classic.

When it comes to comparing marriage to a classic truck, he has a point. We made a lifelong commitment to each other, so this means we committed to the whole adventure. There will be hours of maintenance work, tinkering, breakdowns, meltdowns, blowups, cute photo ops, wear and tear, overhauls, memories, vacations, celebrations, and repairs.

In thirty years, our classic marriage has had its share of moments when we've had to haul ourselves back to "the garage" for work. Our relationship has changed and grown, and like a trusty old truck, it isn't perfect. There is rust, some dents and scratches, worn upholstery, and creaky doors. But it's ours. This is us.

When I think of a classic car show and all the shiny collector models the owners drive to the local burger joint to show off on a summer evening, I don't think it represents real life. These have been painted and polished to look like they did when they rolled off the factory floor. Real life, and everyday use, change a vehicle. Salted winter roads contribute to rust. Along with the memories come dings and scrapes. The new car smell is replaced by the aroma of sour spilled milk and stale French fries. This. Is. Real. Life.

Likewise, a classic marriage doesn't look exactly like it did the day the ink dried on the marriage license moments before you smeared cake on each other—lovingly. A true classic is a marriage that gets the attention it needs and keeps going—flaws and all. It isn't perfect, but it is solid.

We wrote this book to share our story, but it isn't really about us. It's about you, the reader. Look for yourself in these pages. Wherever you are on your journey, figure out what work needs to be done under your hood. Through our story, we hope to inspire others to keep tinkering and working—to fix up what you have instead of abandoning it for something new. And beep the horn when you pass us along life's road, whether in person or on some social platform. We want to celebrate your classic, rust and all!

Michelle and Phil

Forever

Chapter One

A NOVEL ROMANCE

Once upon a time, my husband asked my brother on our first date. And they went without me.

When he finally rallied enough courage to call my house to ask me out, the asking didn't go exactly as Phil had planned. My mother answered the phone.

"Hello," she said in her special telephone voice—the one that could sound happy and sing-songy even when she was in the midst of chewing one of us out. (We've all done that, right?)

In the days before caller ID, texting, Facebook, or email, a boy had to run clearance through a girl's mother before he could talk

> A guy has to take a risk if he ever wants to find true love. *—Phil*

with her. And mothers had a way of making young men believe they could somehow permanently maim a boyfriend with a secret weapon that could penetrate telephone lines—even if their voices were sweet and sing-songy.

I think it was my mother's voice that made Phil think of something profound.

"Uh," he said, punctuating it with a throat clearing. "Um, is Michelle there?"

"I'm sorry, she isn't here right now. She's at work."

Being a think-on-your-toes kind of a guy who rarely makes a plan B, he came up with one on the spot. "Uh, is Brett there?"

"Sure. Just a minute."

Moments later, my brother, who is ten months my junior, accepted Phil's invitation to go to the lake with a mixed group of friends that afternoon. My friends. Not my brother's friends. But of course, he would readily agree to any invitation that got him out of his farm chores.

While the guys settled the details, my mother had a glorious moment of mercy. Apparently, she could see right through Phil's flimsy invitation to my brother, and she yanked the phone from Brett before either young man could hang up.

"Phil, I'd be glad to drive Michelle out to the lake when I pick her up from work at 3:00 if you'd like." That was before I had a license to drive, and I relied on my mother to be my Uber.

> Michelle's mom was nice enough to see through my nerves and realize that when she wasn't home, I panicked and asked her brother to go to the lake with me and my friends instead. Thankfully, her mom offered to bring Michelle out to the lake after work. *–Phil*

Later, I'd wonder if she was the same mother who gave me a 10:30 curfew and allowed me only one date every other week who really made that offer. Now, don't get me wrong, my mother wasn't tyrannical, exceptionally stern, or cruel to us as children. She simply took her role in raising a godly teenager seriously, and that meant setting some strict rules for dating.

I like to think it was Phil's charm that won her over to his side—that

> Hey, asking a girl out isn't easy. The fear of rejection sticks in your head and reminds you she could say no and make you look like a fool. I was worried that Michelle might not have the same feelings that I had, so before I had an awkward phone conversation with her mother, I did what any smart adolescent would do: I had some friends ask her if she liked me. *–Phil*

> I was super nervous that I wouldn't have enough change in my pocket to buy Michelle an ice cream cone. I'd already sweat so much that night with my nerves that when my friends stopped at a store to pick something up, I ran in to buy a clean shirt. Thus, the reason for why I had nothing but change left in my pockets. —*Phil*

and his reputation at church for being the sort of young man who didn't cause mothers undue worry. He attended church and Sunday school regularly, treated adults with respect, and blushed whenever a girl spoke to him.

First Date

Later that evening, several carloads of teenagers headed back from the lake. They were laughing and singing with the radio, and thanks to my mother, I was with them. On the way home, we made a stop at the Dairy Queen.

Phil fished in his pockets for what I would later learn was the last of his change, plunked it down on the counter for the cashier, and ordered one twist cone and one dipped butterscotch cone.

We sat together on a weathered bench with flaking paint under the yellow fluorescent lights of the Dairy Queen awning, oblivious to the sounds of nearby traffic, the mosquitoes snacking on our ankles, or the ice cream making sticky rivulets between our fingers.

In that moment, we were a curly-haired boy who I'm sure was the inspiration for the movie *Napoleon Dynamite*, and a sixteen-year-old freckled blonde girl who could think of little else but the boy brushing shoulders with her—a boy who looked at his own feet more than at her green eyes.

> She didn't know it, but I was focused on her cute little boat shoes and ankle socks because I didn't have enough courage to look her in the eye. And then I got the guts to ask her out on a first date. I was eighteen, and she was sixteen. But in actual maturity, she was more like twenty-five, and I was stuck in perpetual junior high. —*Phil*

At last, he looked at me.

"Do you think sometime . . ." He paused, and then as if something had squeezed him hard enough to force all of the air from his lungs, he finished his sentence with a rapid run of words. "... yamight liketagooutwithme?" He squeaked the ending, like when someone has just inhaled a draft of helium and it's beginning to take effect.

That was the beginning of a romance.

Romance Begins

It's been more than thirty-five years since he asked me out under the yellow bug lights at the Dairy Queen—the same day he took my brother on "our" unofficial first date. Our real first date was to a classic car show. Go figure!

> Romance to me is taking a ride on a motorcycle or hanging out together and her laughing at my corny jokes. It's when she walks by my empty coffee cup and the candy wrappers by my recliner without nagging me about cleaning it up when I'm done watching my favorite History Channel show. Romance is going for a ride in my classic Jeep. *–Phil*

We went to different high schools, and my parents didn't allow more than one phone call to him per week. My parents were smart, but I didn't think so then. Ours was never the flowers and candy sort of courtship. Nor was it the kind that makes for romance novel material.

Ours was a saga of chasing turkeys into their pens together in the rain on his dad's farm. A romance of driving a pickup truck or motorcycle out to dinner and ending up at one of our homes to play checkers or UNO with a little sister. We'd go out for pizza with my family, roller-skating with the youth group, or to visit an antique car show. I wouldn't have wanted it any other way.

Ours is more of a pull-the-engagement-ring-from-his-sock kind of a romance. Yes, that's where he hid it on the night he proposed. I thought he was scratching a mosquito bite.

Could I have held out for a kind of prince charming who would sweep me off my feet the way it happens in fairy tales? Who needs that? He swept me off my feet by treating me with respect. Could he have written me poems and sung ballads outside my window? In a fantasy world. Could I have demanded heaps of gifts and flowers, or something better than McDonalds and bowling for a date night? Not on our budget. That isn't the stuff that makes for real romance anyway.

Can There Be Trouble in Paradise?

Too often, I meet women who talk about how their man doesn't meet their needs. Too often, I thought that way in my early years of marriage. And once in a while, I still think that way until I take my thoughts captive.

Once, I thought romance was a synonym for perfection. But our marriage is far from perfect. And—silly me—I believed that if everything wasn't perfect, the romance was gone.

I'd be lying if I told you the thought of running away and never coming back hasn't ever entered my mind. Of course, it has. I get mad. I throw stuff. I act like a self-centered baby. I blubber and cry. And in the moments before I get rational again, I sometimes think marriage is just too much work.

I had high expectations when we got married. I expected my husband to read my mind and figure me out. I don't know why, since I couldn't figure myself out most of the time.

Our sons and I were reminiscing once when they were teens, and they mentioned an occasion when I had one of my bigger meltdowns. Both said they were sure that night that Phil and I were going to get divorced. Picturing them huddled and discussing that possibility nearly breaks my heart. It was my birthday, and they were in grade school.

I opened the gift Phil had gotten me and held it up. A soft flannel nightgown and matching slippers with Eeyore from Winnie the Pooh on them. I liked them immediately, until I glanced

> Gift gifting is not my love language. Shopping is an idea invented by the devil. I learned the hard way that getting my wife a nightgown that is several sizes too small for her is not a form of flattery. Cheaping out is also not a good idea if it means not getting the right size. Especially if she can't return it or exchange it. My advice to husbands is: you're best off not buying clothes for them. Ever. Slippers, on the other hand, are not the worst idea. Mittens might be a decent choice. Or a scarf. Cash for a massage or a pedicure are smart options. —*Phil*

at the tag. Size medium. I'm an XL gal—like, super curvy. And this wasn't a large medium either; it ran on the small side.

"I might have to exchange this for a different size," I said. I've been fluffy for most of our married life, but I figured he tried to flatter me by getting the smaller size.

"Well, we can't really exchange it."

"What do you mean we can't exchange it?"

"I was in Wal-Mart looking at nightgowns for you when I ran into my sister. She said she had some at home in her gift stash that I could buy from her to give to you. So, I went over to her house."

Suddenly, his innocent mistake wasn't quite as innocent.

"Are you kidding? She knows what size I wear better than you do," I shrieked. "How could you?"

"How could I what?"

"You really don't get this, do you? Both of you betrayed me." I ranted for a long time along those same lines. He never yelled back. (Note: in her defense, his sister is a generous person and always wants to help out her big brother, so even though my feelings were my feelings and I can't change them, this in no way is a criticism of her generosity.)

Eventually, he jammed the offending garment back into the box, tucked it under his arm, and went for a drive. When he came back, he claimed to have drowned the box in the drainage ditch. He remained brooding and silent—a sign he was still angry.

> I have learned that if a husband hurts his wife's feelings, it's hard to get to a place where you want to apologize. I've become better at it over the years, but on the day of the nightgown incident, I wasn't as empathetic as I could have been. I've learned to step back and look at her side of things rather than defending myself. —*Phil*

I hadn't cooled down all that much either. I so desperately wanted him to see how betrayed I felt that he had chosen to get something from his sister's generic gift stash—something he hadn't specifically picked for me. Also, I was deeply wounded about the whole size thing and that I'd received a garment I'd never be able to use.

What was so confusing about the whole thing for Phil was that he didn't get how sensitive I was about my size. He loves me. Fluff and all. Besides, it wasn't as though he had intentionally set out to hurt me. I overreacted to something I could have laughed off as a funny mistake. Although I didn't think so at the time, I had no right to be selfish and ungrateful.

Learning Something About Romance

That event was a turning point for me. I realized how I let my expectations get in the way of enjoying my marriage. I also realized that birthdays, Christmas, and other gift-giving holidays weren't enjoyable for my husband because of the pressure he felt to get the perfect thing to make me happy. He had tried over the years, but he could tell if I wasn't thrilled. One time, he paid my mother to get something. But then I wasn't happy because I knew he didn't choose it, even though I loved the necklace.

> I won't pretend to understand a woman's body image or what her hot-button trigger might be. Just because I love her exactly as she is doesn't mean Michelle sees herself in a positive light. —*Phil*

Our big blowup over the nightgown helped me to see that receiving the perfect gift had nothing to do with romance. I was the one who wrecked the romance with my rant. It had everything to do with my frame of mind. After that, I gave Phil permission to stop shopping for gifts. Instead, we worked out a plan where I choose something I wouldn't otherwise purchase for myself and buy it near the holiday.

We also worked out a concession for the nightgown and slippers after I found the box behind the seat of his truck a week or so later—no he didn't throw it in the ditch. I kept the one-size-fits-all slippers and donated the nightgown to charity. Those slippers remained in my closet for many years as a reminder of my selfish outburst.

It was nearly two decades later when we calmly talked out more of how that whole event made both of us feel. It's important to note that it's never too late to try to understand a painful moment from your past. Talking about it later helped us both gain a greater understanding, far more valuable than our initial fix—no gifts for occasions—had provided.

That removed the expectations and eased the friction, but true healing came much, much later.

Real romance is what we make it. It's experienced in a relationship rather than defined in a dictionary. It's an adventure, not a fairytale.

> Work out conflicts as soon as you can. It took us more than twenty years to talk about the nightgown thing and finally see each other's perspective. Don't be like us. Learn faster. Let go of grudges. *—Phil*

Faithful Marriage

God designed marriage to last. Notice that even when God talks about divorce in the Bible, he never mentions divorce in cases where the wife feels as if there is no romance left in the marriage and her husband doesn't meet her emotional needs. In fact, the word "romance" isn't in the Bible. However, it does talk about love.

In several places in the Gospels, Jesus tells us to love people even if they don't love us back. Tough instructions to follow when our feelings are hurt, aren't they? Consider this passage from the Bible: "No one has ever seen God. But if we love each other, God lives in us, and his love is brought to full expression in us." (1 John 4:12). When we love one another, we represent the love of God to others.

Wives, consider this: how might showing your love to a difficult husband demonstrate God's love to him? How might it demonstrate God's love to your children or others around you? Husbands, how might your patient understanding express God's love to your wife? Even if she's being unreasonable. Especially when she's being unreasonable.

> **Bonus tip for the guys**: don't tell your wife to settle down if you upset her. I used to wonder why certain things made her so upset. But saying, "Just settle," might get your head chopped off, so I'll recommend from experience to keep that comment to yourself. I still might not understand why it bothers her, but at least I have learned to *try* to get it. *—Phil*

If you love someone who is difficult to love, pray for God's strength to show his perfect love to that person despite your own feelings.

Thoughtfulness Equals Romance

> Romance is a state of mind you choose, not something to expect from the other person. Oh, I got all serious there. But it's true. Thank goodness it isn't all that mushy stuff that I'm terrible at. —Phil

Sometimes Phil sneaks into my craft supply cupboard and makes a quick card for me. Isn't that sweet? It's nothing fancy usually, mostly a few hearts or flowers stamped on regular paper with a hand-written note inside from him. I love it! He probably doesn't love that I'm sharing this. But it means so much more than a six-dollar, store-bought card. When was the last time you did something special for your mate? Something that made them feel loved. Here are some ideas to get you started:

- Hide notes around the house for your spouse to find—on their nightstand, by the coffee pot, in their bathroom or sock drawer.
- Send a random text message to say, "I'm thinking of you."
- Leave a sticky note on their dashboard for them to find when they go to work.
- Flirt with each other.
- Make your spouse's favorite treat.
- Give a genuine compliment.

Romance in Everyday Life

Everyday life tests real romance more than anything else. It's easy to feel romantic on a honeymoon, on a weekend getaway, or when deadlines and responsibilities are few. But what about when the harried busyness of real life grips us and impatience grows and

> Great ideas, hon! You could also add washing his Jeep, ordering oil for his motorcycle, and complimenting him on his weed-whacker skills when he mows the grass. —Phil

tempers flare? Yep, that's when it's more difficult to find the romance.

Are there some ways your spouse might be showing romantic love to you that you haven't realized?

Wives, think about the things he does for you. Does he pump up your tires? Put gas in your car? Take out the smelly trash? Maybe he calls you on his lunch break to say hello or brings home a bag of your favorite chocolate when he stops at the home improvement store for caulk and mouse traps.

Husbands, does your wife let you have the remote, even though she would rather watch her sappy Hallmark movie? Does she turn on the electric blanket for you before you head to bed? Does she take time to pack your lunch or schedule your appointments?

Romance is sometimes simply serving each other.

Biblical Love

Romance is love expressed in a way similar to 1 Corinthians 13, the passage read at so many weddings. A person who loves is patient and kind. He or she doesn't do things for selfish reasons or get angry quickly. A loving person doesn't hold a grudge or act out of rudeness.

> She sits on her own side of my truck when we go for a ride, and her carry-on-suitcase-sized purse sits between us in her old spot. But we are still in love. *–Phil*

Phil has shown that kind of love to me for thirty years. We don't hold hands as often as we once did. We don't spend hours gazing into one another's eyes. There are times when we don't like each other as much as other times.

That doesn't sound much like a fairytale, does it? But the romance is very much alive. I've discovered a novel way of looking at romance that reads nothing like a romance novel.

Tune-Up Time

Put away your phones, or if you're using the digital version, turn off notifications and mute your phone, then take a few minutes to talk about this chapter. Maybe you're out on a date. Maybe you're sitting by a campfire or at the kitchen table sharing a cup of coffee—well, your own *cups* of coffee more likely.

- Tell the story of your first date by sharing your memories. Take turns filling in the details. (Phil wants you to know this has to be your first date with *each other*—not your first date ever.)
- Share a humorous memory related to your first date.
- Take turns listing three things that you think are romantic. Do any overlap between the two of you? If not, take good mental notes about each other!
- Dare to go there. Discuss what you think was one of the biggest conflicts in your marriage.

  * How did it end? Talk about it.
  * Do you still have issues to resolve? Discuss those.
  * What would you do differently if you were in that same conflict again?

- What is one sweet thing you can do for your spouse this week? Get out your phone and put a reminder in your notes or on your calendar.

Chapter Two

FIXER UPPER MARRIAGE

*A*vocado? *No, it was more* of an olive that had faded to the color of canned early June peas. The sculptured 1960s carpet covered the floors in all four bedrooms. It was mid-century, but by no means modern.

I stood with Phil in what was to become our new-to-us home and wondered if the decades-old décor disturbed him as much as it did me. Did he notice the sparkly gold epoxy substance that covered all six sides— top, bottom, and four walls—in the master bathroom? Did he feel the urgency to replace the fifty-year-old linoleum? And did he think it odd that even the ceilings were paneled in half of the house? I think he noticed but didn't want to contribute anything to his mounting to-do list.

Despite his apprehension, Phil donned his grungiest blue jeans and flannel shirt and honored my request to bring our new home into this millennium. It's a marvel he didn't recall our previous attempts at wallpapering together in our first mobile home or the time we decided to build a loft bed for our son.

If he had, he might have insisted I stick with the plastic wall tile in the

> Michelle likes renovation more than I do. I would probably live with the paneling and carpet as is. I'm more of a leave-things-as-they-are kind of guy. When she asks me to start a remodel project, I'm usually overwhelmed. I see dollar signs and weeks of work.
>
> Whether Michelle likes it or not, date nights are going to be at the home improvement store. Saturdays will be spent with her coming up with even more ideas while I work on keeping a toilet from falling through to the basement. Subfloors, tile, drywall, and plumbing—there are better things I could do with a weekend. But I love her. And I like it when she's happy. *—Phil*

kitchen, the mismatched counter tops, and the rest of the ugly fixtures.

We spent more than six months on surface renovation before we moved into our home. It was helpful that we purchased it that far ahead of our move so we could spend our weekends fixing it up before we actually had to live in it. We didn't have to tear out any walls or change the main structure, but the results were remarkable. Of course, there was more fixing to do after we moved in. That's a never-ending process. But as I walked through the finished rooms, I rejoiced that our marriage had survived our biggest renovation project ever.

Like classic trucks, homes lose their luster and eventually need improvements. Nothing stays new forever. We've passed our twentieth wedding anniversary, our twenty-fifth, and our thirtieth. And, like classic trucks and old homes, I've noticed that sometimes husband and wife relationships need some surface renovation too. As years go by, relationships change. What was once an endearing quality might be an irritant twenty years later. And the cute little habit of a newlywed may be downright annoying in the mature years of a marriage. After thirty years, our marriage has needed to go through plenty of sprucing up.

Often couples don't think of working on their relationship until they're headed for a major crisis or in need of an extreme makeover type of reconstruction. Some let the relationship maintenance go until they see no solution other than bulldozing it over and walking away. But with a little prevention, it's possible to maintain a relationship in such a way that it can go another quarter century or two without falling apart.

Our circumstances changed in thirty years. We had children. We started snoring. Both of us. We moved three times. We grew up, and our priorities changed. We got wrinkles and sags and started forgetting things. We got lazy and took one another for granted. For our marriage to stay alive and healthy, we have had to learn new techniques for building our relationship.

> Keeping our marriage strong hasn't always been easy; sometimes I don't even like Michelle very much. Oh, did I say that out loud? But I ain't letting this toilet fall through the floor! Huh. Somehow her analogy sounded cuter. —*Phil*

New Subflooring

One of the things we had to change during our home makeover was the subflooring. Before we could put down new tiles, they needed a proper surface underneath. It didn't take an expert to see that a drip from a leaky toilet had caused a significant problem with one of the bathroom floors. Phil assured me it wasn't bad enough that the commode would crash into the basement or anything, but it needed addressing. The rest of the linoleum in the house was chipping and curling enough that we couldn't slap down a new surface without getting the subfloor in better condition.

The subfloor of a marriage is important too. We believe a marriage needs to be set on a spiritual foundation to be strong, and without a solid relationship with God, we would never survive the busyness and overcommitment that have often robbed us of quality time together. But as we've grown in our own personal relationships with God, we have the foundation we need to get through our everyday stresses. Proverbs 27:15 says, "A quarrelsome wife is as annoying as constant dripping on a rainy day."

Yes, many days I can be as annoying as constant dripping. Even as annoying as a leaky toilet. Without choosing God as our subfloor, my nagging and irritation would quickly wear away at any other foundation on which we built our marriage.

Some of the couples we knew from when we were high school sweethearts were married for only a few years before they divorced. They became sidetracked with disappointments and unfulfilled desires. There wasn't a strong subfloor to hold them up when marriage got ugly and broken. It breaks my heart to think of how difficult it must have been for them to go through breaking up. Some couples had no idea where to start, so they worked on surface problems. But that's a temporary fix for a foundational problem.

> I can't imagine our marriage without God in it. Guys, don't make your wife drag you to church like she drags the kids inside at night to take a bath. Step up and go, even if you don't want to sometimes. Your wife might respect you even more if you take the lead spiritually. *–Phil*

When a homeowner allows the subfloor to rot, he can't fix it with new linoleum. If he tries, everything will eventually rot to the point of collapse, even if it looks pretty on the surface for a while. In thirty years, we've learned that a solid marriage isn't built on superficial appearances. A thriving relationship is built on firm spiritual ground.

> Installing a spiritual subfloor doesn't have to be an impossible thing. It starts with one board at a time, and it isn't like it needs to be fancy. A short devotional booklet or app on your phone with devotionals is a good start to improve spiritual habits. You might also consider reading through the Bible in a year with a plan. *–Phil*

Phil and I have built our spiritual foundation in many ways: attending church together, getting involved in various Bible studies over the years, and by using God's Word—the Bible—as our manual for life. We also take time to study the Bible on our own, listen to sermons on the radio or internet, and we enjoy Christian radio and podcasts as a means of staying focused on God. Without Christian friends for accountability, we'd be missing part of our spiritual foundation as well.*

---

* Phil likes the Our Daily Bread app for his devotionals (**odb.org/mobile-resources**), and Michelle likes the YouVersion Bible app (**bible.com**).

There is nothing perfect about what we do, but we keep learning and growing. The way you choose to build your relationship with God is up to you, but it's vital that you do it.

You might be thinking this is easy for me to say since I'm in a relationship in which my husband and I are spiritually compatible. I realize this. I understand that many couples don't have the opportunity to work on their subfloor together because one spouse is not a follower of Jesus. But even in a spiritually unbalanced relationship, if one partner will invest the time to become more like Christ, it will make a difference in the marriage. Is it easy? No. But by doing your part to strengthen the spiritual foundation of your marriage and with the love and support of good Christian accountability partners—spiritually mature friends—it is possible to love and remain committed to a spouse who isn't on the same spiritual ground.

I had a conversation on social media one day with a young woman who was living with her boyfriend. She was afraid that if she took the step of marriage, it wouldn't last anyway. She had seen too many marriages end in divorce and wanted to know how we made it work for the twenty years we had been married at that time. She also wondered what kept me from wanting to go out and cheat on my husband. I didn't use the term subfloor, but I tried to explain to her how our faith was the foundation of our long-lasting marriage.

Committed faith in Jesus Christ holds up our relationship. Because of my faith, I've established boundaries that keep me from getting into situations where I will make an emotional connection with another

> If you aren't connected to other people who encourage you to grow spiritually, that apathy that you feel toward spiritual things will eventually become apathy about your marriage. I grow more when I'm part of a group of other Christians who share struggles and text prayer requests to each other. Going to breakfast with a Christian friend is helpful for me. Accountability over an omelet, bacon, and hash browns never hurt anyone! —*Phil*

man. For example, when I speak at a conference, I won't go out for coffee or have a meal alone with a man. Among my other personal boundaries is the choice not to have an online private chat with a male acquaintance, nor do I ever share any marriage problems with other men. I've made sure, no matter how mad I get at my husband, I will not place myself in a situation where I am tempted to run to another man.

Likewise, because of his commitment of faith, Phil doesn't come home drunk every night or hang out in places where he would meet other women. He chooses not to look at pornography because of his commitment to God and his desire to be a godly husband, and he takes precautions to decrease these temptations.

Having a foundation of faith has caused us to see marriage as a sacred life-long commitment, something not to be taken lightly. Because our faith is interwoven in the decisions we make each day, the positive consequences spill over into our relationship. I long for young people to see how faith isn't a casual, extra element in their lives, rather, it is the pivotal element on which their lives and marriage relationships balance.

Once the faith foundation is in good repair, there is still more work to do in keeping a marriage vital and healthy.

> I like being in my recliner with a cup of coffee, a dish of peanut butter M&Ms, and the remote in hand. But I don't want our marriage to fall apart. So, I've learned how to communicate better–sort of. Modern TV allows me to pause live shows. Win! I can talk with Michelle whenever she asks a question that takes longer than a commercial break to answer! *–Phil*

Refinishing and Fresh Paint

When I first saw the hardwood floors hidden beneath the faded green carpet, years of dirt accumulation and wear marred them. The hand sander removed the damaged surface layer and revealed the beauty of the wood beneath the filth.

There have been so many times in our marriage when I've allowed my grimy selfishness to conceal the beauty of my relationship with my husband. Harsh words I've said in heated moments have left scars on the surface, some deeper than others. Our relationship is always in need of resurfacing through a stripping away of the attitudes and hurts that come from a desire to meet my own needs rather than seeking my husband's needs before my own.

Unconditional love is like a fresh coat of paint that covers over timeworn patience and raw emotions. But somewhere between "I do" and milestone anniversaries, we forget that giving love is required for receiving it. It's natural to react when we're hurt. Anger flares when a husband doesn't listen. Resentment builds when a wife shows too little respect. Criticism damages emotions, and bitterness ruins intimacy. I'm as guilty as anyone of putting my emotional response to my own hurt ahead of loving the way Jesus loves. But I'm willing to keep doing the work to fix it.

Paint and sanding don't cost very much, but they make a huge impact when it comes to home improvement. Most of the improvements to a marriage cost us humility and selflessness; achieving them will cost us our pride, but the results are priceless. 1 Peter 4:8 says, "Most important of all, continue to show deep love for each other, for love covers a multitude of sins." A fresh coat of generous love covers many of our spouse's flaws when we overcome our own self-righteous attitudes.

Updated Wiring and Lighting

Older houses are often a maze of electrical mishaps waiting to happen. In our first little home, we couldn't run the dryer and the microwave at the same time without burning out a fuse. Maybe you've been there.

> Ask your spouse to pray with you. We don't do that as often as we should together. I'm a work in progress too! Michelle has never said no when I ask her to pray together. —*Phil*

"Honey, today is laundry day, so that rules out warming up a frozen dinner for you. We're going to have to order pizza. Again. Oh, and don't turn on the basement light when you grab the clothes out of the dryer because I need to clean up the cereal Junior spilled on the carpet."

The lights dimmed every time I ran the vacuum cleaner too.

We never did get around to fully rewiring that home. We just kept a good supply of fuses on hand. And we prayed a lot about the hidden hazards buried deep in the walls. We ended up making an allowance when we sold the home so the new owners could upgrade.

When we purchased our current home, which isn't much newer than our first home, rewiring was one of the first major projects on Phil's renovation task list. Some of the old wires were frayed and brittle, and several rooms needed more outlets. But before we could add more wires, we had to replace the old fuse box with a new breaker box. The need became an emergency when the dryer overloaded a fuse and started a small fire in the electrical box. Thankfully, the extinguisher was handy. And at least we could use the microwave.

Sometimes a marriage needs a little rewiring too.

After spending more than half of our lives together, our breakers overload a little quicker because of our familiarity and comfort with one another. I'm more likely to lash out at him in anger than I was in our honeymoon years. He's also more likely to see just how far he can push my overloaded emotional circuits before I blow. And he knows which buttons to push. The more complicated life becomes, the more circuits we draw on for power.

> If your marriage needs rewiring, you can't keep adding stuff to the circuit that draws power. If you do, you'll likely have a blown fuse. A fried circuit. A flipped breaker. A fire. We all know what that looks like in a relationship. I've learned that I can't keep letting a problem go, hoping it doesn't blow up. *—Phil*

In our BC (before children) days, neither of us cared too much about whose turn it was to do the dishes or to get up at night with a fussy baby. We ate real food—and not the stuff that came in a box from the frozen food section at the grocery store. We didn't need to vie for the luxury to shop at the mall without a stroller or sit in a deer stand without guilt. Like a breaker with one appliance drawing power, neither of us felt overburdened when only two of us shared the circuit. But when we added two children and more responsibility, we began to overload the circuits until one of us—usually me—blew a fuse in frustration.

> You can't rewire your wife. Wives, you can't rewire us either. But if you're in serious trouble, get an electrician (aka counselor) and start working on your own problems. If your spouse says, "We have a problem," don't ignore it–even if your ego fights it all the way. Fix it. *—Phil*

Where two incomes once kept us comfortable, our decision

to have me be a stay-at-home mom put stress on our financial circuitry to the point of short-circuiting several emotional connections—and our peaceful little honeymoon disappeared in a puff of smoke.

Marriage rewiring isn't a simple mechanical solution. Sometimes, I'd love to rewire my husband to make him think like a woman. And I've wondered if it's possible to install a 100-amp breaker on the compassion and empathy receptacle in his brain. While we're at it, why not add a little alarm that alerts him to pick up his coffee mug and dessert plate from next to the recliner before bed. Or how about a buzzer that goes off when he passes crumpled wet towels and hidden dirty socks. Beeeeeeeeep. "Take note. Laundry nearby."

But then he'd do some rewiring of his own. I think he'd love to replace a fuse box in me that would change the way I react to stress. He'd install a mute button if possible, and likely rewire my libido too. But we can't do those things.

Instead, we can choose to short-circuit our own natural selfishness and choose to put the other's needs above our own. I can choose to love my husband the way God created him. I have spent thirty years trying to rewire my husband when I really needed to change myself first. Our marriage isn't perfect by any means. There are many things we'd both love to improve in our relationship.

> I'm a little scared now that we've been in our house for fourteen years; I worry it's time for more updates. The tiles that I lovingly put on the floor now look old. I look old too. —*Phil*

One area we always strive to rewire is our line of communication. Phil thinks a conversation lasts from one to five minutes. I call that a chat, not a conversation, which I might define in two-digit numbers or even hours. Where he attempts to listen more—even turning off the television when I talk sometimes—I try to shorten my conversations to fit his attention span. It's a give and take.

Of course, it isn't easy. Home renovation isn't without its headaches either. When a pipe fitting broke off during our bathroom overhaul, Phil got an unexpected shower. A day later, the same pipe shot a spray of water in his face and flooded the room again. He didn't appreciate it when I called him Mr. Grumpy Pants.

Like home renovation, marriage renovation also doesn't come without some unexpected roadblocks and stressors along the way. Setting aside one's own needs is uncomfortable, and unlearning old habits is difficult. But making a few changes here and there can ensure that the relationship will make it to the next milestone anniversary, and the next one after that.

Working on our relationship surely helped Phil respond patiently when I suggested we knock a hole in the wall and install a door between the living room and family room. And when I suggested moving the deck from the front of the house to the back. And when I wanted the ceiling fan moved from the dining area to the living room so we could install the free chandelier I picked up at a yard sale—he had to climb up in the attic to tackle that one.

He might not see it the same way, but when I say, "Honey, I think we should rip out that carpet and paint the paneling," I really mean, "Honey, here's an opportunity for us to bond."

Tune-Up Time

Make time to discuss your relationship. If you're reading this book before you are married, this is the perfect time to put together a maintenance plan for the future. Married couples, if you aren't sure where to begin with the renovations you need, making time in your calendar to sit without distraction and discuss these questions is a perfect place to start.

- Describe the craziest renovation project you have ever tackled together.
- What role does faith play in your relationship right now? If you could make a change, what would you do differently?
- If you are not yet married but preparing for marriage, list at least three ways you could establish a foundation of faith before you get married.
- If you have been divorced and are remarried, you can't change the past; letting regret consume you isn't helpful either. You're accountable for what you do from this point forward. How could a foundation of faith make a difference in your present marriage?
- What do you think you could try that would improve your communication and your closeness to one another?
- In what ways do you think your ideals might be unrealistic?

- What is the number one thing you and your spouse argue about?

  * What step do you need to take in order to move toward resolution for this problem?

- Name three day-to-day issues or responsibilities that you think have worn on your relationship as years pass by. After each one, list a way you might be able to renovate your thinking about it in order to have a long-lasting and committed relationship.

Chapter Three

JUST MARRIED

There were quite a few years where Phil and I felt as if we were just married—not the newlywed honeymooners sort of just married. I mean we were simply married but not thriving. It happened sometime between the birth of our first child and when that child left for college. We will talk more about how parenting affects marriage in chapter 5, but I think it's possible to be "just" married, even if you never have children. It's a symptom of what happens when the "new car smell" fades in a relationship.

When I got my first new Jeep, it had that smell for a short time. For a brief moment there were no scratches on the cranberry red finish and there were no stains on the seats. But then someone dinged me with the door of their monstrous SUV. And then I bumped into the cart rack at Target. (It was a teeny-tiny scratch, but a certain someone noticed it right away!) Then I dropped some chocolate

> New car smell is overrated. It smells like car payments to me. *—Phil*

on the seats—*that* was inevitable. Not long ago, we had to replace the tires, and suddenly it isn't new anymore.

When does the new marriage smell wear off? Maybe we lost track of "us" while we were tracking cross-country meets, baseball games, basketball, forensics, and trombone performances. Perhaps the drift took place in the middle of one of our moves to a new home and a new job—we had two of those. Or maybe it was earlier than that. It gradually happened. Then one day, it didn't feel the same as it always had.

I think back to when we were dating and we counted down the days until we would see each other again. Or when we were engaged and it felt like forever until we would finally have the wedding and move in together. Yes, we did it in that order. We both committed to waiting until we were married to live together and to have sex. That might sound ridiculously old fashioned, but it was part of our commitment to the importance of a covenant in marriage. We will talk more about a covenant in chapter 16.

The Way We Were

As established in chapter 1, we started dating when I was sixteen and Phil was eighteen. While that might sound like a recipe for an immature relationship, there were many things about our young relationship that I have observed in people who marry much later than we did. Okay, I'll admit that some of my letters to Phil were notes folded up like paper footballs on pages torn out of my biology notebook. Remember making those? I was so concerned about all things high school, and he was so concerned about all things fun and social. But does age have all that much to do with it? I've seen couples of any age who display the same characteristics:

- Thinking of each other all day long.
- Sending thoughtful letters—a more modern version is texts, emails, Snapchats.
- Carefully dressing and grooming for time spent together.
- Complimenting each other and expressing appreciation.
- Doing thoughtful things for each other such as holding the door open, running an errand, or washing the car.

- Sacrificing for each other by going to a restaurant the other person likes, even if it isn't our favorite.
- Sharing everything, even half of our favorite candy bar.
- Spending hours doing almost nothing but being content to smile at each other, hang out, and hold hands.

> I used to mail love letters to Michelle when she was in college. I think I wrote sappy stuff. Do we have those somewhere, hon? Maybe we should burn them. —*Phil*

After a Few Years of Marriage

As time goes on, doesn't this become more familiar?

- Thinking of what annoys us about his or her habits.
- Sending text messages that say, "Did you remember to take out the trash? It really staaank this morning."
- Throwing on some dirty sweats and a ratty shirt, wearing a pony-tail in hair that was washed three days ago, not shaving (his face/her legs), and not being overly concerned about the "air" that we give off.
- Giving a peck on the cheek (if there's time) and brushing off holding hands because one of you says: "I'm texting right now" or "Wait 'til I'm done posting to Instagram."
- Expressing disappointment and frustration over nitpicky items.
- Leaving dishes in the living room for her to clean up; borrowing his cordless drill and running down the battery, then forgetting to put it away.
- Insisting on going to the all-you-can-eat meat buffet even though she's vegan, or insisting on eating at the world's best salad bar when he hates all things green, then saying, "Deal with it."
- Hiding all of the best candy where your spouse will never find it. Eating up his Easter candy while he's at work.

Are you getting the picture? It doesn't always work this way, but it's pretty typical. We get in a comfortable place and slowly change our habits and let go of the behaviors that once spoke to how much we value the other person.

Old Married Couple

Have you ever noticed that we refer to "young married" couples but rarely, if ever, to "old married" couples? And yet, after thirty years of marriage, I'm thinking

> In our first weeks of marriage, I would eat, put the dishes in the sink, and then go to work on a little model Ferrari I was putting together at a card table in front of the TV. She gave me a crazy-eye look.
> "What's wrong? This was how it worked in my family. My mom took care of that stuff."
> (In Michelle's defense: we lived in a mobile home park and I had nothing to putter with in the garage. It was winter. And we had a garden shed, not a garage.) So, I started to wash the dishes after supper. —*Phil*

we must qualify as old married by now. Over time, it isn't that I have loved Phil less. I've shown it less. I've let my needs bump up over his, and suddenly I'm all about me. And it happened in the first five years of marriage!

I don't know when I morphed from doing full make-up, coordinated jewelry, perfectly styled hair, and an outfit selected after trying on six of them all the way over to greasy hair, dry shampoo, stained sweats, and the mugshot look. It just happened. I knew it was a problem when I put on makeup and styled my hair, and one of our young boys asked me, "Are we going somewhere?"

"No. Why?"

"You look all fancy."

If by "all fancy" he meant I had one look for leaving the house and another for staying home, he would be correct. That was a wake-up call saying I needed to find a balance between mugshot and tramp. Combed hair, a touch of eyeliner, a clean shirt, and a little lip gloss became my new casual look.

The guys aren't off the hook either. There are things they let go of once they secure that diamond on your finger. Since 1985, Phil has been holding doors open for me and getting the car door for me when I get in.

It's his way of making sure I'm safely tucked in my seat and no purse straps or limbs are dragging along when he drives away. I like it. He doesn't do it because I'm helpless but because he respects me and cares for me. He isn't particularly nurturing or doting in many other ways, so this is one way that expresses something that matters to me.

> When we were dating and talked on the phone for hours–more like we fell asleep on the phone–I counted down to our wedding. But then, she started to complain about my bow hunting. What's up with that? –*Phil*

The other thing I appreciate is that he doesn't make a habit of "letting one rip" in my presence. He will never belch the alphabet either. Thank goodness! If these things endear you or impress you, that's fine for you. I know there are guys out there whose sense of humor includes wafting a belch in the face of their wife or trapping flatulence under the bedcovers and then puffing it her way with a flap of the duvet. Whatever floats your boat, I guess. But if she doesn't like it, would you consider stopping it and finding a new way to amuse yourself?

Despite all of my struggles with self-image about weight, Phil has always told me I am beautiful and never said one thing about my muffin top. He has been baffled about the things that unintentionally trigger my sensitivity in this area and been clueless about what to say when I'm in the depths of self-loathing. But he has not made me feel less-than or ashamed of my size. That has come from within me.

> Chewing noises give Michelle anxiety. I didn't realize what a complication this might become when two people sit down for a nice meal at a quiet table. Until our children came along, we often ate in front of the TV to help cover up the sounds of smacking, chewing, and gulping. –*Phil*

Aging isn't always kind to couples either. Hair turns gray or goes away altogether. Leathery skin, age spots and wrinkles replace smooth, youthful skin. Potbellies, saggy breasts, and lumpy thighs show up and make themselves at home. My biceps have turned into bingo wings. But when we have a love for the

> I wish women had temperament buttons on their foreheads that would indicate their mood as they approach. Like a mood ring, but more obvious. Or maybe an alarm meter that talked. "Warning. We are three sarcastic comments away from blow-up." *–Phil*

character qualities—and more—of our spouse, the physical things don't repulse us. They're physical qualities, but nothing more. I often look over at Phil and think he looks more handsome now than when I first met him. Well, not when he's snoring in the recliner and his mouth is gaping open, or when he flops his head around like a slow-motion bobblehead doll, but when he's driving the car and I glance over and admire his hair. Or when he smiles at me across the room.

As I navigate through menopause, it throws new challenges in our path. Whoever said teenage girls were moody and emotional didn't live with a woman going through perimenopause—to help the men understand, this is the term for the process of going through menopause. It's an era of unpredictability for the relationship of a couple. It's hard to say which mood might show up each day.

One day a chatty and chipper cheerleader offers to make coffee and breakfast, and the next day a nitpicky nag might show up in her place. "Get yer own," she barks. "What is this, a Denny's?"

With hormones and cycles all over the place, there are times I'm feeling amorous and others when I'm prickly. Phil says I'm like a cat. I have green eyes, so maybe I'm a cousin to the felines. I want to cuddle on my own terms. One day he can give me a hug, and the next I might try to

> Meow. If she's a cat, I'm clearly a golden retriever. *–Phil*

scratch his eyeballs out. Okay, not literally. But if you've ever seen a moody cat swing her paw at a passerby who never even made eye contact, you know what I'm saying.

Where Do We Go from Here?

We don't need to be "just married." If you're just married right now and longing to be happily married or thriving married, there is hope. It has taken us some time to work through the struggles. We're still working through a lot of them as they pop up. But I can say we are in a better place now than we were even five years ago. Don't give up!

We attended an eight-week program at our church when we had been married for twenty-seven years. At first, we didn't sign up because we figured after this many years, we had arrived at "as good as it's going to get." As if that's a destination. It's more like where you arrive when you lose the GPS and guess your way from New York to California.

I was willing to settle for what we had. And a few years prior to that we had done a video series together. I learned some things from that but didn't put a lot of what I learned into practice. We had done other books and series, too, not because our marriage was crumbling, but because we wanted to make sure it didn't. Usually it was my idea to do these things.

So, when Phil said he wanted to do this eight-week class, I said I would make arrangements to leave work on time to get there every Monday. I wasn't going to ignore his request. Each week, couples watched video segments over dinner (a table for two) and then discussed the content with the use of a workbook. Some parts of the whole thing seemed cheesy, but it was mostly because of our own awkwardness with the process of learning how to listen to each other and respond.

It wasn't easy to seriously discuss some things in a room full of other people, either—even with the background music playing to cover up our conversations. And there was homework. That meant we had to

> One way that I make my wife happy is by turning up the heat in the bedroom every night. I mean I literally turn up the heat in the room and put on her heated mattress pad. She appreciates toasty warm sheets. What did you think I meant? –*Phil*

> I don't usually like to speak in front of people–ever–but at the end of the eight weeks, I was willing to get up on stage and give a testimony to the group that my favorite homework week from the program was the one about sex. Michelle says I'm "sooo junior high." –*Phil*

> I have chosen to love my wife even though she wants to wear noise blocking earmuffs while I chew, she insists that I leave the toilet seat down, and she leaves dishes in the sink now for *me* to take care of.
>
> She loves me despite my dad jokes that have more cheese than an order of nachos and my obsession with looking at classic Jeeps on Facebook marketplace. Being an "old married" couple is pretty sweet. *–Phil*

discuss more at home, where there wouldn't be witnesses in the room to keep us calm.

This is when we discussed several things we had hidden away for years, and we made some progress. Was it a little bit uncomfortable? Yes. A lot. But it was worth it to make our relationship stronger. And I didn't have to cook dinner. Plus, Phil made me laugh. It broke through our "good enough" and helped get us moving toward something better.

If you aren't sure what your next step is, I encourage you to use the discussion points and activities at the end of each chapter. If you haven't already started to use them, you can go back and use the ones you missed. Pick and choose one or two to try. From there, you might decide you need to attend a conference for couples. Maybe you'll need to see a counselor to help you talk through things in a safe, controlled way. Too many couples skip this step because they feel shame over needing help.

All of us need help. Once we admit it, we can each start to experience a better marriage than we thought possible. Phil is an excellent car mechanic, but even he has times when he needs to take a vehicle into town to have someone—with more skill than he has, or who has a new perspective—pop the hood and run diagnostics. Even couples with marriages that aren't "that bad" can sometimes use the help of an expert, or a seminar, or a book.

The kind of love that keeps couples together for the long haul isn't the kind they make movies about. In the movies, a couple who is in love might be portrayed through steamy sex, the inability to keep their hands off each other, mid-day passion, and more sex. But strong and long-lasting love has more than just sexual passion. It has faithfulness. It has kindness. It has patience for the messy stuff of life. They seldom make movies about that. It isn't glamorous or even interesting.

Who pays to see movies about people who wash the dishes for each other? Or about men who clean up dog puke at 5:00 a.m. because an aging prostate prompts a trip to the bathroom, and they don't want their wife to step in barf when she gets up for work. Who writes romance novels about saggy, wrinkly bodies? The heroes are always ripped, with oversized biceps and six-pack abs. The heroines have bikini bodies and long flowing hair. They smell like violets and musk.

> If you compare your life–your wife–to the movies, you're in for a disappointing show. A little side note: I do think the movie *Napoleon Dynamite* may have been based on my life story–seriously my senior picture from high school proves it. I feel the need to say, "Vote for Pedro." —*Phil*

Real life—real love—is beautiful, but not always pretty. It is not always happily ever after, but it is filled with happy moments. Love isn't a whim; it is a choice. Why settle for "just" married when you can choose to pursue the best marriage you can possibly have?

Tune-Up Time

- Take turns listing some of the thoughtful things you did for one another when you were dating.
- Which of these do you still do now?
- What about your early relationship do you find silly now?
- If you have some of your old love letters to one another, read a few for a grin.
- For fun: what movie (old or new) do you think represents your relationship?
- If someone were to make a movie about your relationship, what would you call it?
- On a scale of 1–10, with ten being the most willing, how willing would each of you be to seek help from a counselor for your marriage? Take turns sharing your number.
- If your answers were vastly different on the previous question, without interrupting, allow for each of you to state your reasons for your answer.
- What will be your next step to work on your marriage? Will you attend a retreat together, seek a counselor, read a book, take a class? Write down your next step and sign your names to it.
- List several non-physical qualities that you each love about the other.
- List several physical qualities that you each love about the other.

Chapter Four

THE MARRY-GO-ROUND

Have you ever hopped on a merry-go-round on a playground and then had someone spin it as fast as they could? Step back in the recesses of your memory and listen to the squawk of the rusty metal. As the rotations come faster and faster, one lap blurs into another. Recall the dizzy head and being on the verge of losing your lunch, your arms like rubber bands that have lost their stretch and are about to snap. Remember the feeling of being so much at the mercy of the person doing the spinning that you have no choice but to hang on for dear life—or risk a traumatic injury by letting go. That's how marriage can feel sometimes too. Like a marry-go-round instead of a merry-go-round.

We can't always control what happens, and it feels like we're about to be sick. We call out, "Stop the ride!" but it keeps spinning. So, we hold on. On a merry-go-round, children scream with delight. On a marry-go-round, couples simply scream.

Most of us don't start out on the marry-go-round, although some start out on a slow spin. For example, if yours is a blended family, you probably started out with tracking schedules, planning weekend visits, carefully choosing where to sit at sporting events and recitals, and managing kid discipline when "you're not my mom." Or here's another scenario: if you were both college students when you got married, it might have been a bit crazy as you balanced labs and study groups, part-time work at the deli, a cleaning job, a couples' group at church, and visits to extended

> Merry-go-rounds make me puke. We were still newlyweds when I rode The Zipper at a carnival and ended up in bed for three days from the vertigo. I can't believe I *paid* to ride it. —*Phil*

family. Most couples start out with a plan for advancing their careers, buying a home, living a relaxed suburban or rural life, and socking away money for retirement. There is so much on the ride that they can't see as it blurs into the whirling background.

They don't expect companies to close and layoffs to happen. They don't anticipate a health crisis, taking care of their parents, or a child with special needs. They don't sign up for bankruptcy, lawsuits, car accidents, cancer, or affairs. These things happen, and suddenly the ride spins out of control. Some can hold on and survive. Others let go and endure the bruises, pain, and scars that come from lurching off the ride.

Never Say Never

I have heard the phrase "never say never," many times. I'm not superstitious, so I have no thought whatsoever that by saying I'll never do something, somehow that makes it happen. But I do know that when I dig in my heels and say never, God sometimes has this way of pressing me to see if I really mean it. Often that comes in the form of an opportunity to do the very thing I said I would never do. So, I find it a little crazy that I still think I can plan out the next twenty years and have it happen just so.

For example, I said I would never stay home with children. And I didn't want them until I was at least thirty. Before I even graduated from nursing school, I had signed a contract to work as a cardiac nurse and accepted a nice bonus from the hospital in exchange for my three-year commitment. They had a fantastic daycare at the hospital, so I figured our future kids would someday go to that daycare. My career was on track to make a lot of money.

But at twenty-two years old, I got a fever I never expected.

Baby fever.

I tried a puppy. That didn't work for baby fever, so now I had baby fever and a puppy—one with anxiety and behavior problems to boot. It wasn't even a full year into my career, and I certainly wasn't anywhere near fulfilling my contract. But there was nothing that was going to fix this fever outside of giving birth to a human.

> I didn't love that dog. Sadie should have been named Satan. —*Phil*

Phil agreed we could start trying to get pregnant. Turns out, "start trying" was code for "you'll be pregnant by your next cycle." We were on our way to starting our family.

I continued with my plan to use the hospital daycare. But in mid-pregnancy, around my twenty-third birthday and around the time when we needed to pre-enroll in the daycare, I decided I wanted to stay home when the baby arrived. We had planned for this possibility—I thank God we had the foresight for that at our young age—by purchasing a home that we could afford on one salary, in case something were to happen that would turn us into a one-income family.

At the end of my maternity leave, I cut my hours to casual on-call hours at the hospital and worked a few days each month. Then I had our second son at age twenty-five and turned in my resignation letter.

I had said I would never leave my career to stay home, but I did. And it was right for us. But that one change spurred all sorts of other changes. For example, my income was two-thirds of our family income at that time. When

> Owning a house and having babies means you need more money. We didn't have much of that. But we chose to have less money and have Michelle stay home with the kids. I chopped a lot of firewood to avoid having to run our propane furnace, which I think was manufactured when Lincoln was president. It mooed when it was warming up. Like a big old heifer in the basement. Maybe it felt the financial pressure too. —*Phil*

you chop up your financial security like that, something has to change. Luxuries such as cable and eating out had to go. This was pre cell phone and internet, so those weren't a concern. I learned to shop at garage sales and discount stores for clothing, and while I love shopping at these stores, I still couldn't cut enough to stay afloat financially. There were times when there was more month than money.

When finances get rough, husbands and wives fight about money. I think I just heard you say, "True dat." And when finances are rough, there is no wiggle room in the budget. Which can lead to more arguing. This means that if breastfeeding doesn't go well, there is no money for formula. I hadn't factored in this problem.

Breastfeeding was supposed to work. It was free.

On one income, we would qualify for a program our state has for women and children that gave vouchers for formula and other nutritious foods. After my vacation pay ran out and maternity leave was over, I had a choice: go back to work full time or apply for the program.

I applied. And I struggled with the stigma every time I went to the grocery store. I don't think less of any woman who chooses to work when she has children. I believe we can all choose what is best for us. And I thought what was best for our family was for me to be home. So, I swallowed my pride and took the vouchers.

One day, I was in the checkout line at the grocery store and using my vouchers. Back in the day, before benefits like this were loaded on plastic cards to be scanned like a credit card, mothers received separate checks for specific items. The grocery clerk had to ring up each set of items on its own receipt. So, I would group my items: the milk and cereal with its voucher, formula with its voucher, and cheese and peanut butter with another.

This was particularly annoying for anyone who ended up in line behind me, as it meant waiting for four transactions to

> When I was single, my mom packed me a PB&J sandwich, a little bag of sour cream and onion chips, Little Debbie snacks, and a Mountain Dew for me to take to work. I was twenty-three and carefree. But when I became a married man, and then little people joined our family, suddenly there was all this pressure. —*Phil*

be rung up. As I bounced my baby, I turned back to look at who was in line. Right behind me was one of my former nursing school professors who had been my clinical instructor. She immediately asked me why I wasn't working. Not, "You aren't working as a nurse anymore?" Another person to chastise me for "throwing away my career." I don't even remember what I said, but I know

> Late night Home Shopping Network shows while taking a turn rocking a colicky son left me a zombie at work some days. Tired people are irritable–it affected both of us. –*Phil*

I was grateful when the groceries were bagged and I could run away from this unpleasant scrutiny and conversation.

By the time I started to adjust to living within our means, baby number two was on the way. On the day his dimpled little cheeks entered the world, we didn't know he would turn out to be colicky. Within two weeks we knew. That lasted for his first year of life. And the marry-go-round spun.

When Austin was six months old, we finally tried a getaway with the two of us. Shortly after we left town, Dallas, our two-year-old, decided to hop off the footrest of the recliner at Grandma and Grandpa's house and landed in such a way to snap two bones in his left arm. And then while the cast was still on Dallas's arm and more medical appointments were still on the calendar, a new job offer came along for Phil, but we had to move there within a month. Thirty days to pack up a family of four and sell a house that badly needed repairs, all while potty training a kid in a cast, keeping a house neat enough for a real estate agent to give tours, managing a fussy baby—and the marry-go-round got another giant push.

Shortly after the move, my mother was diagnosed with ovarian cancer. She was forty-seven at the time. She now is a survivor of over twenty-five years, but that year was a blur of treatments, complications, my dad selling their farm—and the marry-go-round spun faster.

What Spins Your Marry-Go-Round?

You don't need a play-by-play of our whole life story. The idea is that with each push, life spins even more. We have different circumstances, but the push is there just the same. Marriages fall apart sometimes when it's too difficult to get past the strain and stress.

In the Tune-Up Time at the end of this chapter, you will have the opportunity to look at some of the inciting incidents in your own life that have led to stress in your marriage. Acknowledging them and looking at how you coped is a great way to begin slowing down the spin of the marry-go-round. Even if you're long past an incident, the fallout can still be there. If you coped in an unhealthy way, then it might have set off a pattern of unhealthy behavior that damaged your marriage. Perhaps it was a wound that left such deep scars that you chose to put up a barrier in your relationship, and you're merely roommates now.

Whatever it is, there can still be healing. It might be painful to dredge it up again, but if you can press the reset button as a result, then the pain will be worth it. Let's talk about some things that have helped Phil and me survive the ride.

Tips for Coping

- **Make time to relax.** When Austin was at the peak of his colic, I would leave him with Phil for a few hours so I could go to town. But I soon realized that if it only involved shopping, this would add to our budget stress. So, I started going to the library. Sometimes I would sit and look through books there. Sometimes I would check out a stack to bring home. It was a brief time to relax.

- **Make time for each other.** This will take effort. Even if it's only a short amount of time, it's important. Let's imagine your time is spent caring for a parent in your home. At the end of the

> Not all rest or recreation has to be with each other, as long as you both agree on the arrangement. When our boys were small, I would go canoeing in the wilderness with my dad every summer for a week. Now I go with the boys. Michelle has gone to women's retreats with girlfriends. I work to clean up the house while she is away so she can come home to a restful environment. *–Phil*

day, you're exhausted and have very little interest in anything but unwinding in front of the TV and sleep. But even thirty minutes spent in conversation about your day—without the TV—can bring you closer to each other. I remember when Phil would come home from work, and while he took a bath, I would sit on the toilet lid and tell him about my day caring for preschool children.

- **Cling to each other over others.** This sounds obvious, but when life feels like it's spinning, grabbing each other and holding tight isn't always our first response. Sometimes we grab for other relationships or for unhealthy coping.
- **Make a reminder list of what you love about your spouse.** I have a list of things I like about my husband that I keep tucked in my Bible. Every so often it falls out during my morning devotions. It's a great list to have when I'm frustrated with him for something that probably isn't his fault.
- **Get on the same page.** Talk about the details that are taking place in your life. Discuss how to handle circumstances, plan your next step, and problem solve. You are a team. Rather than playing against each other, shoot for the same goal.
- **Spend time in the same space.** For the first half of our marriage, we lived in small houses. There's a country song I used to listen to about love growing best in little houses with fewer walls to separate.[1] It's true! When you're forced to interact by proximity, you work things out. You talk more, sit closer together, and do life together. The more separated we are in how we live, the more intentional we need to be about being together.

When the Spinning Stops

I have discovered that "crazy" is a season. Like spring, summer, fall, and winter, crazy doesn't stick around forever. But be prepared. You have probably heard couples say they drifted apart, or they grew apart. Like the centrifugal force of a spinning merry-go-round, which pulls outward, many couples are spun away from each other. It's possible to hang in there through the worst of everything, only to realize when the spinning stops that you don't have anything to say anymore—nothing in common, apathy about your relationship, and no desire to stay married.

This is similar to what happens with some parents when the kids leave home and they face an empty nest. Empty nest syndrome is a real thing. All of our efforts might go toward launching our kids and celebrating their achievements, but when the time comes that it's just the two of us, what happens if we aren't sure we even know each other anymore?

New Connections

When our boys left home, Phil and I started the process of reconfiguring who we are. We're still working on our marriage—intentionally. Rather than setting life on cruise so we can coast, we set our sights on another hill to climb, another challenge to make our relationship a priority. How that looks for you is probably different from how it looks for us. But the important common ground is the mindset: we agree to continue to grow and change.

Another outcome of a changing season is realizing that conflict can lead to growth. It teaches us something about ourselves if we're self-aware enough to notice. If you look for your own character flaws rather than scoping out your spouse's, you might get an education about what you could change. When you take a good look at your attitudes and reactions, you can ask yourself, "If I saw these qualities in my spouse, what 'helpful' advice would I feel obligated to dish out?"

If you can apply that advice to yourself, you might be surprised at the outcome. When we focus on changing ourselves rather than on changing our spouse, it's amazing how much better the outlook appears.

> Our life has slowed down some since our boys got married. But we can't figure out why it's so hard to find one night each week for a date with each other. I am thankful that Michelle is still my best friend. Laughing together has a lot to do with making the marry-go-round more fun. I like to make Michelle laugh. With dad jokes. —*Phil*

Tune-Up Time

- Discuss what makes your relationship sometimes feel like a marry-go-round.

  * Which of these challenges do you both have in common?
  * If you could make a change, what would be a first step to slow down "the ride?"

- What has been the hardest challenge you have had to face as a couple?
- If you have had a traumatic event that damaged your relationship, how do you feel about it now? Do you think you have worked through it and found resolution?

  * If you still have work to do, discuss what you think your next step should be.

- Do you think you're too busy? On a scale of 1–10 with ten being the most busy and one being the least, how busy do you feel your life is right now?

  * What, if anything, would you change right now?

- Brainstorm a list of date activities that both of you would enjoy. If funds are limited, come up with free or low-cost ideas. Include some that require little effort or planning for the crazy weeks.

Family

Chapter Five

MEN BEHAVING DADLY

"*It looks like a grenade* went off down there."

Those were the words that began our parenting adventure as Phil and the doctor had a little fraternity party at the end of the bed while I pushed my eyeballs out of their sockets bearing down with massive contractions. The point was to push a baby out of my bottom, but that wasn't progressing as well as the party between the only two guys in the room—unless you count the one that was the real center of attention. But we didn't know his gender yet.

While nurses held a leg on each side, and the doctor attempted to artfully create some sort of suture-able episiotomy in my nether regions (men if you're reading the long version, you'll have to look up episiotomy if that's a new word), there was a camaraderie of the brotherhood that I didn't understand happening between the two men waiting to catch our eight-pound, thirteen-ounce, cone-headed blessing.

In their defense, we had all been working on the process for nearly eighteen hours—well, I had been working, and they were pretty much observing. Also, in Phil's defense, tactfulness has never superseded an opportunity for him to make a joke, so I should have expected this.

"Will you have to give her a transfusion after this?" Phil was not about to give up on the momentum he had going.

"Hey guys, over here. I can't feel my legs. Have you noticed the nurses? I'm a puppet without strings right now." I was grateful for the epidural but had to watch the contractions on the bedside monitor and wait for the tightening sensation in my back to know when to push. Sometimes epidurals do their job too well.

> When I first held Dallas, all I could see was his cone-head. "Is this normal?" I asked the doctor. My next thought was, "I'm responsible for him." I know it doesn't sound manly, but it was instant love to hold our fist son. Michelle got to carry him for nine months in her body, but this was my first opportunity to really touch him. And I loved him instantly. *–Phil*

A few more snips and a couple of pushes, and Dallas, our first baby boy, finally entered the world. This was the start of testosterone domination at our house.

"Is this normal? Will his head stay like that?" Phil has always loved asking questions to which he already knows the answer.

Two years later, on the same day, and within the same hour, baby boy number two was born. Austin (no geographical affiliation on the name choices) completed our little family of four, and I decided that if God blessed us with sons, I didn't need to keep pumping out kiddos until I got one with pigtails—no disrespect to families who have more than two, or even more than ten children.

With both births, we had the option of having Phil spend the night on a cot in the hospital, but if we chose this option, the baby also had to stay in our room. I opted to let daddy drive home, even though it was the wee hours of the morning by the time my stitches were finished, I'd had some toast and applesauce, and we were ready to settle down. We decided the nurses were exceptionally qualified to watch babies all night, and I desperately needed some sleep.

I also needed to let my eyeballs recess back to where they belonged. I'm sure my crossed eyes weren't as noticeable as it seemed they were to me. I wanted a root beer and to sleep for a hundred years. At least I got the root beer.

Marriage After Kids

No parenting book ever really prepares a couple for what children do to a marriage. There are extensive books available to explain what to expect while pregnant and what to expect in the first year. They cover spitting up, constipation, prepping the family pet, lactation, snake bites and spider bites, and babyproofing. But they miss a lot.

> After having the first baby, I didn't think I could love another one as much as I loved the first one. I had the same instant love reaction the moment he was born. —*Phil*

Where are the chapters on falling asleep as soon as you try to watch a movie together, children barfing in the sheets of your bed, getting parental sleep in two-minute increments, and the impossibility of losing the baby weight while surviving on hotdogs and frozen pizza?

For dads, where are the CliffsNotes on receiving zero attention while your wife smooches the cheeks off your spawn? Or on precisely how much touching stay-at-home mommies can tolerate after a day with the kids? And where are the books on being patient when daddy wants to go hunting, but mommy is a raging hormonal maniac who doesn't trust herself for one more minute with your mini-me?

That's when real life smacks us upside of the head. That's when marriages can make it or break it. We made it, but we ended up "just married" for a while, as already covered in chapter 3.

Parents pour every bit of love into raising the children, helping them feel secure, getting them to appointments, school, social events, and lessons. These are difficult years. But too often, couples abandon each other, thinking there

> While Michelle was pregnant, I had the unrealistic idea that having a baby wasn't going to change my life much. It's like having a puppy. Michelle would take care of him. Maybe it's a delusional thing so that dads are willing to have kids—if they knew it would change their life as much as it does, they might not want to venture there. —*Phil*

> I took my turns getting up in the night, and because we were feeding bottles, I was able to have that close time of holding a baby, feeding a bottle, and watching the Home Shopping Network. *—Phil*

is another, easier option. They separate, meet new people, get married, have more kids, and then realize they're right back to where they were before.

Stress Means Mess

Childrearing isn't the only life situation that puts strain on a marriage. For some couples, infertility creates a shift of identity that makes it difficult to move forward together. For others, a devastating career crisis spins one spouse into a season of depression and discouragement—a time of pushing even a significant other away. Serious illness presses pause on plans and leaves a lot of what-ifs. I don't want to minimize those scenarios, and we will cover some of them in coming chapters.

Let's pause here to focus on only what parenting can do in a marriage. It's okay if you choose to skip this chapter because you aren't a parent, but if you read it, you might gain some insight to use when counseling a friend.

BC (before children), I experienced baby fever whenever one of my friends brought a new bundle of joy into the world. There is this maternal instinct that kicks in when a woman holds a baby. No matter what friends tell us or how many times we see YouTube videos of babies having diaper blowouts or well-aimed pee fountains or poorly timed spit-up incidents, and no matter how sleep deprived our friends look, there comes a point when many of us think our life will never be complete without a child in it.

The process of making a baby is fun—most husbands will agree. So, they will readily comply with a wife who insists they must up the ante on their frequency of sex during the

> Having a newborn means you rarely get the bed to just you and your wife anymore, you're going to take some of the smelliest bags of diaper trash out to the garage, and you get pretty efficient at cleaning up throw-up off the carpet and furniture. *—Phil*

pre-pregnancy phase. Girlfriends, I think this is equal to shooting ourselves in the foot with our own weapon. We increase the frequency right before pregnancy, delivery, and needy babies. Isn't that a bit like putting a cookie in front of our husband, letting him have a few bites and then snatching it away and tossing it in the garbage while he watches?

> Babies change your sex life. I don't want to scare any guys who are reading this. But your wife might be touched out by the time you get home from work. Little people get the best of her affection sometimes. —*Phil*

I'm generalizing here. I know it doesn't work this way for every couple. But if husbands are reading, I have a feeling they agree. Without offering any excuses for why this drop of frequency occurs—I understand it 100 percent—let's think about how your guy feels. First, his friends have probably talked with him before you had children. Some of them warned him this might happen. But he hoped against hope the two of you would be the exception. And he doesn't understand what this has done to your body and how your boobs hurt and leak constantly. He doesn't understand why your libido is low, but you still want to have a second child, even after seeing how it's going with the first.

Put yourself in his shoes for a moment and empathize. Yes. Let's have a moment of silence for the life we used to have.

When we can set aside even legitimate reasons for our own struggles and see how they affect someone else, it can open the door for a conversation. It can break down defenses and walls.

> We definitely want our wife to at least empathize with our needs. And I can't speak for all guys, but we will try to not be insensitive idiots. (Try is not Michelle's favorite word. She and Yoda would be great friends: "Do. Or do not. There is no try.") —*Phil*

Our children were out of the house before I could clearly communicate to Phil that when I'm "not in the mood," it isn't because he repulses me. When we get to the chapter on intimacy, we'll address this again, but for now, open the door to considering how having children has affected your husband's world.

> I will admit I wasn't always as understanding as I could have been with Michelle. Instead of withdrawing and feeling as if she wasn't attracted to me, I could have spent some time thinking about her struggle. Emotions don't affect a guy's ability or desire to experience intimacy with his wife.
>
> But it doesn't always go that way for her. Be patient and talk together. I wasn't good at communicating my feelings. Work to get your eyes off your own needs and consider how you can love and support each other. —*Phil*

Lest husbands think they are off the hook for empathy, I want to put it out there that there are no words to adequately describe how your wife struggles with wanting to make you happy and to see the look that says, "You are my princess," in your eyes.

But she also has little ones hanging off every limb, a schedule she has to manage for four, or five, or maybe seven people. She needs to be more creative with the food budget and the ever-changing taste buds of toddlers.

The laundry has multiplied. The noise in the house has quadrupled. She optimistically thought she had the stamina and calm focus of a super mom, and she's wrestling with her disappointment in herself some days. And now if she wants to have "special time" with the daddy of her children, little ears down the hall and little feet at the door add to her inhibition and take away her free-spirited delight in your couple time.

That doesn't get better when they turn into teenagers who are very aware of what moms and dads do when they love each other.

Solutions

The most important concept to remember in raising children together is that life as it is right now is temporary. There will be some days when your needs aren't met, some days when you get all the wrong messages from each other, even when neither of you was mad at the other.

You will have to divide your time and attention with other people. But there will be other moments where you look over the head of a child and share a grin together about the behavior you know you have to discipline right now, but it's oh-so-funny and you don't want your child to know that.

There will be days when you check your attitude and press forward in love. I hope there will also be moments when you really admire each other for how you parent your children together. I love watching Phil with our boys. Over the years, we made so many wonderful memories with them.

> Dads, be involved in raising your children. Enjoy the time you can spend feeding them, wrestling on the floor, changing diapers, tucking them in bed, or reading a book. It isn't all your wife's job. I don't regret being a hands-on dad. I think that being involved when they were younger is what made it so much easier to talk with them as teens and now as adults. —*Phil*

It was when Phil was doing the dad things that I had such tenderness in my heart for him. It was when he wrestled on the floor , tucked them in bed with his snug-as-a-bug-in-a-rug tradition—sometimes even when they were teenagers—that made me admire his dad skills.

Or when he talked on the phone with one of them when they were away at college and they shared their own laugh about something. It's when he spends his whole weekend off working on one of their trucks, or when they come home as adults and stay up talking late at night with Dad—those moments remind me that we chose to marry each other because we each had qualities we admired then, and we still do.

If you're in the middle of parenting and losing touch with the heart connection between each other, it's still there. Your hearts are tethered to your children, and through that strand, you are tethered to each other. Someday, the kids will leave home. If you suddenly find yourself holding the loose end of a rope and look over at your

> Take notice and appreciate how your wife takes care of your children and how she pours herself into their needs. Notice how she sacrifices her own hobbies or even career to care for them. Michelle left her career as a registered nurse to be home with our children. —*Phil*

spouse, who is holding one too, it means you just launched an adult into the world. Tie those loose ends together again and rediscover the joy of who you have always been as a couple.

What Not to Do

When we're in the middle of raising kids and discover that the stress of it is getting to us, there are some important things not to do:

- **Don't withdraw.** When Phil felt rejected by my lack of attention, he would often withdraw to protect his own feelings. That withdrawal made me also feel rejected, which made *me* withdraw too. That wasn't healthy for either of us, and we were both equally responsible.

- **Don't lash out.** In our hurt, it's easy to say something we might later regret. Again, empathizing about what the other person is experiencing will help to set aside the selfish feelings about how MY needs aren't being met.

- **Don't look outside of your marriage for a relationship.** Doesn't this seem obvious? Maybe. But it seems that when we withdraw from our spouse emotionally and physically, it tends to lead toward reaching out to someone else who will show us attention and listen to our needs. But it never makes anything better!

- **Don't talk about your spouse's shortcomings with someone else.** Work it out together. Even if you want to talk to your best friend, start by talking to your spouse first. Or at least be guarded about how much you share with a friend before trying to work it out with your spouse. If your husband doesn't help as much with the kids as you'd like, talk to him about it, not to your mom. Guys, if your wife isn't intimate as often as you'd like, that isn't something she wants your best buds to know.

- **Don't put your conflict on social media.** Deep down inside, we know this isn't a good idea, but I see people do it anyway. It's like saying, "Here. I haven't shamed you enough with my angry words; let me invite some more people into our life to publicly shame you."

If I could offer some advice to **men**, I would encourage you not to make your wife the enemy if you don't think your physical needs are met exactly as you'd like. Work it out with her. And whatever you do, pornography is not a substitute or a fix. *—Phil*

If I could offer advice to **women**, I would want you to understand that when testosterone kicks in, our brains pretty much go into a one-track mode, which gives us magical blinders and we can't see the toys on the floor or the kids that need baths. We don't see the spit-up stains on the front of your shirt. We're oblivious to the teenagers up the hall. *—Phil*

Tips for What to Do

Do we wish we had done more of the right things and fewer of the wrong things for our relationship? Of course! But no one gets through thirty years of marriage by doing everything right. It's about learning from our mistakes and doing it better the next time conflict happens.

- **Pull together.** Team up and serve each other, rather than looking for ways to be served.

- **Give each other a break.** Phil and I both have our separate circles of friends. It's important to find time to relax with them too. Guys, watch the kids without thinking of it as babysitting. Please. It's never babysitting when they call you Dad. It's parenting. Girls, let your husband go fishing without a guilt trip or being overly needy.

- **Get away together.** It only happened once a year or so when our kids were little, but we would leave them with Grandpa and Grandma for a weekend and go away together. Hold hands, talk about your dreams, and do couple things—yes guys, I mean sex—when you have the opportunity. I'll admit that on a few of our getaways, I was too emotionally exhausted to have any desire for romance, and I regret that. But I'm thankful we stayed in the habit of going away together.

- **Express your admiration for each other as parents.** I appreciate when Phil tells me I am a good mom. He appreciates hearing that I respect him as a father to our children. Thank each other for the tasks each does. Praise a good parenting move, appreciate a moment of tough discipline, or compliment a funny solution.

- **Be a team.** I can't express how much I appreciate when I know Phil has my back. I have often been the firmer disciplinarian in our family, which means he is the fun dad. I have asked him in the past to defend me when one of our boys was disrespecting me. Likewise, Phil needs me to not undermine his decisions—even if it was chocolate cake for breakfast or banning vegetables at supper while I was away for some time with my friends. When the fun police are away, the fun dads will play.

I have so much respect for parents who come through raising their kids and still like each other and want to spend time together. It's a big job, but you can do it and still love each other deeply in the process. How it looks for each family will be different. So rather than compare, let's cheer each other on to marriages that last!

> Every marriage is different. We'd love to be able to offer the perfect formula that would make you feel as close to each other after having kids as you once were before them. Mostly, it will take a commitment from both of you to figure out your formula. Hang in there and love each other. —*Phil*

Tune-Up Time

- Describe what a perfect day would look like in your marriage.
- Discuss how your marriage has changed since you had children. What was the most surprising change?
- If you could change anything about the current state of your relationship, what would you change?
- If you don't yet have children, what do you think your life will be like when you do? What do you think will change?
- Take turns listing several things that you appreciate about each other as parents. Intentionally give out compliments.
- What do you value most about your relationship with each other right now?
- Tell your spouse one thing that you really need from them right now that would help you feel more secure in your relationship as a couple and as co-parents.

Chapter Six

YOUR DNA IS SHOWING

In Phil's family, Jell-O was a dessert. In mine it was a salad. His family ate dinner; ours called that meal lunch. My mom folded bath towels in thirds. His mom folded them in half. In the scheme of life, these are minor things. But in the middle of a tense marriage moment, they might become a battleground on which someone is willing to risk their life to prove they are right. In our case, that's usually me. Our families of origin and their unique traditions have an impact on our own marriages.

> Dinner is in the middle of the day. Haven't you heard of a dinner pail? —*Phil*

In both of our families, our parents had lines of distinction when it came to husband and wife duties. I saw my dad run the tractor often as a child, but don't recall seeing him run a vacuum cleaner until I was an adult—not counting a shop vacuum. It wasn't that he wouldn't, it was simply a task my mom always did. She also did the dishes and cleaned the bathrooms. She tended the garden for the summer after he tilled it up each spring.

I do remember a few times when my mom was working the evening shift as a hospital nurse that my dad took care of us. His large hands would fumble with the pins on my sister's cloth diapers and he struggled to get the rubber pants back over her chubby, kicking legs. Dad would warm up whatever Mom left us for supper, but she prepped everything before going to work.

Once, he fed us chili and then my brother threw up right before bedtime. I remember wondering who was going to clean it up since Mom wasn't there. My dad gagged his way through cleaning up barf, and that memory is still etched in my brain. But if my mom was there, he didn't jump to take on such things.

Phil's dad went to work at the paper mill and came home each day to do the chores on their mini-farm and his mom took care of the cooking, cleaning, and laundry. Phil lived at home until our wedding and had a close relationship with his mom and his dad. He baled hay with his dad and tinkered on trucks and tractors. He did dishes with his mom and ran the vacuum for her. She still packed Phil's lunch every day for work and washed and folded his clothes right up until the day we got married.

> I'm not embarrassed to admit that if I hadn't gotten married, I might be still living with my parents at age fifty-three. That, or in a van down by the river. When I lived with them, my only bill (yep just one) was the payment on my 1987 powder blue 4x4 Dodge Dakota. And my mom packed some pretty sweet DINNERS for me every day. Did you read chapter 4? I mentioned them there. *—Phil*

Imagine Phil's surprise when we got married and I didn't get up in the morning to pack his lunch. We hadn't talked about this before the wedding. It wasn't on the list of details to work out in advance.

> Dinner.

Suddenly, here we were with an unexpected situation. Phil is an easy-going guy, and after a little ribbing about my "duties," he jumped in and took care of packing his own lunches. On a related note, I do not pack his suitcase when we travel. If he forgets his toothbrush, I don't want that to be on me!

Not every couple can resolve the who-does-what dilemma with ease. I know there are husbands who insist that their wives pack their lunches and their suitcases. Some wives will do the task without complaining and will do it with genuine joy. Others (more like my M.O.) would do it if asked, but there would be a lot of resentment packed in with the other stuff. They might let it become a barrier, yet they won't be bold enough to discuss it with their husband.

It's important to discuss the differences related to expectations that are rooted in the traditions of your family of origin. Communication is the best way to work through it and settle on a system that works for you—not the one that works for your parents but for the two of you.

Understanding Multiple Points of View

Phil's mom and I had some rough patches in our relationship. These also stemmed from traditions and practices from our own families. It takes time to get to know one another. One area where we were different was in how often mothers and daughters (or daughters-in-law) talk to each other by phone. When I left home for college, I didn't talk to my mom every day. I didn't even talk to her every week. She wrote me letters, and I called home sometimes, but I was quite independent.

On the other hand, Phil's mom talked to her girls every day—sometimes more than once per day—when they were in college, into their married years, and beyond. My mom and I have a good relationship, but we don't need to talk every day. It really isn't in my personality. But for Phil's mom, this is what made her feel close. So, when I received daily phone calls from her and sometimes more than that, I felt smothered, and we had tension in our relationship. "I don't even talk to my own mom this often," I thought. "Why do I need to talk about every life detail with my mother-in-law?"

I was young and didn't think

> Some of us grew up as momma's boys—not saying that was me or anything. Marriage puts one guy in the middle of two women who love him. It makes it easier if they can learn how to get along. Some of our wives grew up as daddy's girls. A husband has a hard time competing with a perfect guy. —Phil

through these differences very well until later. Rather than noticing that this was her attempt to feel closer to me and to treat me like a daughter, I perceived it as her checking to make sure I was being a good wife. I withdrew from her and asked Phil to answer the phone more often.

Looking back, I know I could have handled some things differently. We never had an open chat about what either of us needed. I take a lot of the blame, yet I know it goes both ways. Especially now that I am a mother-in-law myself, I realize I also need to understand my daughters-in-law and their needs and boundaries. Communication can clear up so many misunderstandings.

I wish I had been mature enough to see more of her side of things and had discussed with her how different my relationship was with my own mom. I would have tried to help her understand that I'm more of an introvert who needs space. Space to me doesn't equal rejection. But to Joy, I think it did. I was in my thirties when Joy passed away after a battle with cancer. I wouldn't mind having an opportunity to do a few things over again.

The problem with in-law conflicts is that they put us in the middle between parents and spouse. In the case of Phil's mom and me, he didn't want to hurt either of us, but he was stuck in between, and it became a source of marital tension when he tried to please everyone.

Family Differences

There are many sources of conflict that could potentially arise based on the traditions in your family of origin:

- Will we spend or save our money?
- Will we have a joint bank account?
- How will we do vacation? Do we go somewhere together as a couple, take separate fun trips with friends, or a combination of both?
- Who will work outside of the home? Both of us? One of us?
- Where will we go to church?

- What is our style of communication? Do we confront issues right away or sulk and withdraw? Do we work it out? Blow up? Suppress our feelings?

- How will we celebrate holidays? What will be our new traditions as a couple?

- How did our parents handle conflict? How will we handle conflict?

- How affectionate were our parents? How affectionate will we be at home?

- Will we discuss topics such as sexual satisfaction openly, or is that something we're not comfortable with?

> My family discussed many topics openly that other families might not. When I was in first grade, my sister said, "Do you know how babies are made?" This was right after my parents had brought my younger sister Diana home from the hospital. Laurel made me promise not to tell my mom that she had told me this secret info.
>
> However, in total shock, I went straight to my mom to ask her if it was true. My mom wasn't quite ready for this question. She didn't deny it, but the look her face confirmed all I needed to know. —*Phil*

I come from a family that doesn't talk publicly about sex—not even clean jokes—and we don't openly discuss topics such as menstruation, puberty, sexual dysfunction, and the like. You can imagine my shock when I was visiting Phil's home when we were dating, and his dad said, "Jo, let's take a bath."

"Wait. So, your parents take a whirlpool bath together?"

"Yeah. Why? Is that weird?"

I promise, I'm not sharing any family secrets; the kids shared a photo of them, with faces peeking out of the bath bubbles, on the slideshow at Joy's funeral for the entire church to see.

It also wasn't weird for their family to find creative ways to share the one bathroom they had in their house. For example, if Phil was in the shower and his sister needed to use the toilet, she would pop in the bathroom and go while he was behind the curtain. They had to be finished with their business before the person on the other side of the curtain turned the shower off and needed to reach for a towel.

It also didn't matter if someone locked the bathroom door in an attempt at total privacy because any butter knife could turn the lock to open it from the outside. They had their own version of privacy, and it worked for them.

> Laurel got in a little trouble for sharing the shocking truth of the birds and the bees with me, but that didn't stop her from getting out "the book," which explained reproduction with chickens and eggs and then progressed to the explanation of human reproduction. This openness was normal in my family. We asked questions. We got answers. –*Phil*

At our house, we didn't share the bathroom. We learned to be fast when everyone finished farm chores. I took a quick shower and then went to my bedroom to do hair and makeup. In. Out. Next person.

This is probably why I have never cared about having a master bathroom with double sinks. I am not fond of brushing teeth together or trying to style my hair while Phil brings the bathroom humidity up to 95 percent with a shower hot enough to steam broccoli.

My parents have always been affectionate with each other, but never inappropriately—meaning, it was never awkward or uncomfortable for us as kids. They still hold hands after fifty-two years of marriage. They always hugged and kissed in front of us. Phil's parents were that way too.

There are subtle differences between what is normal in each family. When you get married, you have to make a new blend of normal for your household. Every generation is a new mix of relationship genetics. When our boys got married, they took our family blend and then brought it to their own marriages. This is starting to sound like I'm talking about

Amish friendship bread or sourdough starter. In some ways, that's exactly what it's like.

Our characteristics, good or bad, carry into the next generation. Even silly habits or unusual traits. More than once when they have been home for a weekend, Phil or I have done something and one of our daughters-in-law has said, "That's where he gets it," about one of the boys.

Family Dysfunction

Our genetic makeup does affect our marriages, but the environment in our family of origin has even more to do with it. Even our familial sense of humor, quirky habits, code words, and responses are all part of what I think of as our DNA: Distinctive Native Attributes. No, that isn't what DNA really stands for. There's some huge scientific term to go with that. But we're going to think of it as our distinctive native attributes here.

Whatever dysfunction you had in your family growing up doesn't necessarily come into your own marriage. But it does affect it. If your father was an alcoholic, you might have different ideas about how much is okay to drink. If your parents' marriage ended because of an affair, there might be a bigger challenge to establish trust in your own spouse. If you were physically or emotionally abused as a child, the scars are still there. If you were sexually abused and stuffed away the trauma, old memories might surface in vulnerable moments of intimacy. The emotional chromosomes for shame or hiding, abandonment, denial, fear, distrust, and avoidance might be part of the DNA you bring to the relationship.

If one or both of you were raised by a single parent, or if you divided your time between two households, had stepsiblings, stepparents, or lost a parent to death, you might have some post-traumatic stress related to your experience. All of these influences affect how you perceive your own relationship. For example, if your father left when you were young, you might have a fear of being abandoned, and you become overly attached, even clingy, in your marriage.

We bring good DNA too! The distinctive native attributes we possess can include our fun quotient, sense of humor, creative conflict management, caring, compassion, empathy, joy, etc. These are all part of our DNA makeup as well.

Leaving and Cleaving

Your families are a support system for you, but as a married couple, your first priority is to each other. This can be hard! Especially if you have an exceptionally good relationship with your parents. Or if your parents depend on you to help with their needs—a business, a farm, physical or health challenges.

The Bible talks about leaving father and mother and clinging to each other. The verse is found in Genesis 2:24, and it was established with the first marriage in the world—Adam and Eve's. In older translations, this verse is worded as leaving father and mother and "cleaving" to each other. Cleave isn't exactly a word we use every day, but you may have heard this phrase used at a wedding. Interestingly, Adam and Eve didn't even have a family of origin, yet the instruction was already given. Who will argue with an instruction from God that has been around since the first couple got married?

> Whatever the situation, we become one when we get married. I'm a maintenance guy, so let's try a little example here: we're like epoxy or JB Weld. Once you mix the two elements, there's no going back. It's a permanent bond. *–Phil*

Marriage is a special bond. It is like no other. You didn't get to choose your parents. You had no say over whether you were born, how many siblings you have, or how functional your family would be. But you do get to choose your mate. Unless you were part of an arranged marriage, you chose each other, and when you wed, you believed you were ready for marriage. Oh, wasn't it fun to discover how unprepared you really were?

As we learn to be a couple, it's important to leave behind our single lives. Leaving doesn't mean abandoning. It means shifting our first loyalty to each other. This takes intentional effort. It means discussing something with each other first, rather than bringing our parents into the mix.

For example, if Phil does something to upset me, I want to discuss it with him first, rather than confiding in my mom. I want to fix it together, not drag others into our business. It means that we can get love and support from our families as a single unit, not as two singles.

Phil woke up on the morning of our wedding in his bedroom at the top of the stairs in his parents' home with a dog and cat beside him. He went to the church, said his vows, headed to the reception with me, and then we drove off on our honeymoon. His leaving all happened in one day. That was hard for him! On the other hand, I had more of a transition period. I left for college just after turning eighteen and lived away from home for a good part of the next two and a half years before our wedding day. Each time I returned home to my parents' farm for summer break, I felt more and more separated from their everyday life.

Leaving means separating physically—moving out and sometimes moving away. It also means separating emotionally, relationally, and financially. If one of these steps hasn't yet happened, I'm willing to guess it's the source of some marital conflict.

> **My math**: avoiding conflict = avoiding conversation.
> **Michelle's math:** talk + listen = solutions. Hers works. —*Phil*

Tough Love and Solid Marriage

If your parents are more involved in your relationship than they should be, are you brave enough to loosen your ties with them and grow your bond as a couple? They might not need to be as involved in your relationship as they are. Is there something you've never talked about that has eroded your unity as a couple? We know how painful those conversations can be, but they are also productive in bringing you closer together.

Is there pain from your past or some misperceptions that stem from your family of origin that have hindered your progress in becoming unified as a couple? Your DNA is showing! As you look at each of your distinctive native attributes, practice showing consideration for each other's differences while you honor what you both bring to the relationship—good and bad. Why not go out for lunch together while you talk about it?

> *Dinner.* Go out for dinner together. —*Phil*

Tune-Up Time

As you discuss these statements and take next steps, it might be painful at first and produce some temporary conflict. But if you commit to the process of opening communication, your marriage can be better than ever before.

For each of the following statements, say whether you agree or disagree. Then discuss why you chose your answers. Rather than defending your own answers, listen to one another and try to rephrase what you hear your spouse saying. Agree or disagree:

- I am sometimes uncomfortable with the behavior of my spouse.
- It is hard to express my true feelings to my spouse.
- Sometimes my spouse really hurts my feelings.
- I feel as though my spouse honors and respects my family of origin.
- Our families have very different cultural (social/economic/ ethnic) values.
- My spouse is too dependent on his or her family.
- I am comfortable when around my spouse's family.
- I think my spouse's family (my in-laws) value me for who I am.

Chapter Seven

NO CHICKS IN THE NEST

When our firstborn moved into his dorm, it felt odd to drive away and leave him there with a few crates of his possessions, a small refrigerator, and a pile of brand-new sheets and towels. Having only one child at home was an adjustment. Two years later, when we packed up our second son to head off to college, it felt even stranger.

We were the only people to pull in on college move-in day with a motorcycle on a trailer—something Austin didn't want to leave home without. A group of hulky football players surrounded our minivan as soon as we stopped at the unloading zone, and in the same amount of time as college-aged boys can polish off a pizza, they had emptied the van and carried everything upstairs— except for the motorcycle. We unloaded that in the parking lot.

> Shouldn't everyone take a motorcycle to college? *–Phil*

Phil and I drove home with an empty van and an empty trailer. That felt weird. It also felt weird to walk past bedrooms that stayed clean for weeks at a time. We discovered that we cannot consume a gallon of milk before it goes sour—something that hadn't been a problem for twenty years.

For nearly two decades there had been kids in our nest. Then they were half in, half out while they went to college. And at last, the nest was empty. For the first few of years of marriage, it was just the two of us. It's odd to think back to when we could plan a weekend based on what we wanted to do together.

We would talk about someday and wonder what our kids would be like. Now we're looking backwards with satisfaction, but it's a little like when you plan for a trip and it finally comes. Then the last day of the trip arrives. And it's over.

Parenting never really is over, but it is different. But before we talk about kids leaving home, let's talk about couples who have not had children. That affects a relationship too, and many books about marriage assume that married equals parent when it comes to status. This isn't always the case, whether by choice or circumstance.

Empty nesters—a term that usually applies to couples whose children have launched into adulthood and left home—aren't the only ones with an empty nest. No matter the situation that has brought them to a place where there are no children living in their home, each couple needs to seek out ways to keep their marriage strong, whether it's for a season or long-term.

No Kids Yet

Some who are reading this book are hoping to have a family someday. Some have been trying for a long time, and now you're wondering if time is running out. Others haven't reached the point where they are quite ready. If that's the case, you're still figuring out how to deal with the impolite question, "So, when are you guys gonna have kids?"

> When she said it was just the two of us for the first years of marriage, I think Michelle forgot about our little cocker spaniel that was the spawn of Satan. We had to find puppy sitters for her every time we wanted to go somewhere.
>
> –Phil

If you're waiting, you might be experiencing stress based on which of you wants to have children sooner. Or you may have conflict over when you'll be financially ready. Perhaps your relationship didn't get started on solid footing, and you've realized you need to work on that before bringing a baby into the mix. Or you may be blissfully happy and not ready to start a family.

If infertility treatments are part of your weekly routine, you've probably discovered how this can affect your marriage. There are emotional, physical, and sexual implications in that process, including the stress that comes with trying and waiting for results, hoping, being disappointed, and trying again.

In this season where your nest has not been filled, I encourage you to do these two things:

- Make time for each other. Even if this isn't a stressful time for you, make time while you have it! Believe me, I don't think we really thought about the implications of waiting twenty years to be uninhibited again. Children are never a burden, but we might have relished and savored our alone years with deeper appreciation.

- Focus on being a team—ignoring what other people say. Your decisions about the timing of your family are up to you as a couple. It is no one else's business.

No Kids by Circumstance

Whether you found out before or after your marriage that you will never be able to have biological children, that has an effect on your relationship. Perhaps you were able to get pregnant but then miscarried. The pain and unfulfilled hopes of multiple miscarriages is so deep. I grieve for those who walk this path.

Maybe you have struggled to find a place of agreement on whether to continue treatment or to consider adoption or foster care. If your body image has changed and social gatherings are difficult, you may be feeling the effects as a couple. You may have lashed out and argued about "whose fault" it is. Your bank account may have taken a blow for the sake of treatment that didn't end up fulfilling your dreams.

Some couples have lost their only child or children to illness or tragedy. I can't even imagine that pain. If you've had to bury the only children you've ever had, I have no adequate words to express how sad I am for your loss. What heartbreak you have gone through.

Some marriages don't make it through this kind of pain, so if you're still weathering it together, this is a gift. In this season:

- Grieve together. Talk about the dreams you've said goodbye to. Cry. Process at your own pace without telling your spouse how they should feel.

- Talk about your fears, anxiety, and disappointment. Give expression to the feelings you might stuff away.

- Find joy together in something you both appreciate. This means finding new ways to connect that are not related to fertility or children.

- Reach out for support from family and friends or a counselor.

- Make a difference. Find a cause that pulls at the heartstrings for both of you and enjoy the satisfaction of making a difference for someone else.

No Kids by Choice

The number of couples who choose not to have children fluctuates, according to Pew Research,[2] but it is a real demographic of the population. In many Christian circles, there is a stigma and guilt attached for couples who choose not to have children, as if having them is the only God-approved choice. They are labeled as self-centered, and there are plenty of articles out there that will claim this is sin. I don't agree with those articles, but the purpose of this discussion isn't to debate that.

Along a similar line, we've had some criticism for choosing to have only two children. We knew we were done when we were done, and we've never looked back and wished we'd made a different choice.

The operative word is choice. This is a choice that is between the couple and God. It is no different than choosing to wait one year, or five years, or ten years before trying to start a family or choosing when a family is complete. For couples who choose to have as many children as the Lord wants to give them without the use of any birth control, that is their choice too. But let's be cautious about declaring that one or the other is the "biblical way."

My call to everyone reading this chapter is: let's love and support each couple in following the path that God has given them. I don't know why we feel strongly about someone else's decisions in marriage, but it happens. Yes, God has said children are a blessing from him, and procreation is part of the mandate for humanity at large, but nowhere does the Bible say every married couple must desire to have children.

If you have chosen not to have children:

- Communicate well. Know how each of you feels about the decision. Allow for the freedom to second guess it if that should come up. Talk about the social pressures and how that makes you feel.

- Reconnect with each other to make sure you don't live separate lives. After many years without the responsibility of juggling schedules for kids or parenting, your relationship is much freer than some. It might be easy to drift to a place where you live parallel lives. Be intentional about staying connected.

- Devote yourselves to something that makes a difference for the kingdom of God. This doesn't mean you have to become pastors or missionaries, but find a cause that brings you together. Why? Couples with children are usually united by the mission of raising kids. If you commit together to a cause that unites your hearts in serving, it can challenge your marriage in new ways and bring you closer.

No Kids Because They Grew Up

If you're here with Phil and me, welcome to the club. We had a temporary stint with telling our boys what to do, but now their wives have taken up that torch. They might come to us for advice about big decisions, but they make those decisions with their own spouses. We have a loving relationship with them, but we have released them to adulthood.

There is a certain amount of sadness that comes with this phase as well as a certain amount of glee. In their high school and college years, Phil grew an especially close bond with our boys. They made many memories doing "guy stuff" such as canoeing in the wilderness, fixing cars, binge-watching Marvel movies and *Lord of the Rings* (the extended version for crazy over-the-top fans), and other stuff that made me retreat to my room with a book.

> Dads, learn how to text. Some of my friends refuse to learn how to text. It's a great way to stay connected with our kids. *—Phil*

They had inside jokes—about me. I enjoyed deep conversations about life and spiritual things with them. I loved watching them become men. But when the time came for them to officially move out of our house and into their own home with a wife, I had the easier time saying goodbye. Fly little birds, fly!

For Phil, the score is back to even now. For a while, I was outnumbered. He enjoyed a little frat party with boy behavior, and he always had someone to laugh at his jokes. But now, it's all on me, the audience of one. I don't always think the same things are funny. See chapter 12 on that. The carefree club that he enjoyed with the boys changed when girls entered the picture and rightfully asked for a claim on their time.

For me, it has been a journey of starting to reclaim some of Phil's time, which speaks to my love language—quality time.[3] I try to be empathetic toward his sadness in watching two of his best buddies move out.

I'm thankful that over the years, we didn't lose "us." Phil and

> You may have thought that for all these years, she wanted you to come home every night to relieve her of kid duty. But consider this. Maybe your wife wants you to be her friend, not the babysitter. When our boys first left home, I worked longer in the evenings on my projects and hobbies, or stayed late at work, treating the independence like a reason to do my own thing. I'm learning that Michelle–whose love language is quality time–really likes me home. *—Phil*

I are still friends. We still like each other. That isn't always the case for empty nesters. But you can get back some of what you once had. You both will need to be vulnerable and willing to take a step toward each other. You might have to knock down a few bricks that you built between you over the years.

Phil's grandparents were married for more than seventy-five years. If that is how it will be for us—Lord willing—that means we have another forty-five years together as empty nesters. Yikes! That's more than double the number of years we have been married so far. Life is far from over. But many marriages don't survive this phase because when the common cause of raising children ends, so does the reason for staying married.

> Twice as long? Wow.
> Love you, babe.
> —Phil

If you're an empty nester, here are some ideas to help you weather another thirty, forty, or fifty years together:

- Rediscover your friendship. Have breakfast together, play a game, go for a walk, or go to a movie. I love to sit by a campfire in our back yard and toast marshmallows with a catch-up conversation. It is possible to feel lonely even when you're together, so make ways to connect in everyday life with meaningful conversation. You may have spent years talking only about the kids, so this might feel awkward at first. Give it time and effort, and you won't be disappointed.

- Nurture one another's dreams. What did you put off so that you could put your children first? As a mom, I put some things on hold in order to be with our kids as much as possible. But moms aren't the only ones who experience this. Many times, a husband will forgo a career change or a dream in favor of the financial stability his family needs. It isn't too late to earn a degree, launch a business, write a book, or change careers.

- Figure out what works for you with a balance between time together and time with friends. I want Phil to hang out with guys. That way, I don't have to laugh at *all* of his corny jokes! I know I keep mentioning that, but it really is a thing—his jokes. And I don't have to watch endless seasons of *Meat Eater* or *Mountain Men*. You now have the freedom to do some things on your own without worrying who will make sure the kids are fed and get to baseball practice. I have taken trips to visit my sister in California, and Phil goes on fishing trips with friends. We also take at least one long retreat together—a tradition that we started at our twenty-fifth anniversary when our kids were in college.

- Don't be too proud to get counseling. Just because you've been married for a long time, it doesn't mean there is no use in seeing a counselor! If you *do* have a potential forty-five years ahead of you, why not make those wonderful years? Many couples see a counselor regularly as a preventive and not because they have any big conflicts.

- Find a new hobby that you both enjoy. It might take some experimenting to figure this one out, and I've learned that it's important to have a positive attitude in the exploring process— or at least try to have one. We know for sure that wilderness camping isn't our couple hobby. I don't have anything close to a good attitude about that idea, so we scratched it off the possibilities list. We talk more about this in chapter 9. However, we've discovered that we both love hiking, and I like taking photos of pretty scenery. Phil is patient about going on walks in the woods that involve frequent pauses for me to fish my phone out of my pocket and snap a picture of something to share on Instagram later.

> With only two of us at home now, I can concentrate more on Michelle. I'm not as distracted. Well sometimes . . . when I am not on my phone. Facebook marketplace has a lot of really cool old trucks and Jeeps. —*Phil*

- Start a Bible study for empty nesters and build friendships with other couples in the same life phase. Hanging out with other couples helps both Phil and me to feel less isolated and reminds us that all couples have challenges.

Whatever the reason for why it's only the two of you in the house now, you have an opportunity to have a thriving marriage. As you navigate through physical and libido changes, grief, depression, loneliness, or disappointment, practice being tender and understanding. Your first instinct might be to push each other away. Pull closer. Hold on. Patiently make your spouse's best interest your priority. Above all, put on love, which binds everything together in perfect harmony (from Colossians 3:14).

Take a good look at your wife. She's still the woman you met thirty-something years ago. Having no kids listening in on disagreements is no excuse to spill out years of all the unhappiness you saved up. Choose your words wisely. —*Phil*

If you're looking at the next forty years and that sounds like all of the worst options in a game of "Would You Rather?" you should probably do something about that. Seriously. For example: Would you rather spend an afternoon with your wife or have someone pull out all of your nose hairs one by one? Would you rather eat a centipede or go out to dinner with your wife? Yeah, find a good counselor or meet with your pastor. They can help you figure out your next steps. —*Phil*

Tune-Up Time

- Describe something you've always dreamed of doing personally.
- Describe something you've always dreamed of doing as a couple.
- What are the barriers preventing you from achieving these dreams?
- What has been most difficult for you in your current season? (No kids yet, grieving over loss, no kids by choice, empty nesters, etc.)
- If you're hoping to have children but don't yet, what is something you'd like to do before you have a baby?
- What fears do you have related to parenting and your current season? (Having children, foster parenting, adoption, raising stepchildren, launching kids into the world.)
- If your nest is empty or nearly empty, discuss the plans you have in place for the next season of your relationship. If you haven't made plans, start a dream list.
- If you could do one thing from this chapter that would help you grow closer together, which one would you do?

  * Focus on being a team.
  * Volunteer together.

* Communicate more.
* Grieve together.
* Rediscover your friendship.
* Nurture one another's dreams.
* Balance time together and with friends.
* Get counseling.
* Try a hobby together.
* Start a small group with other couples.

- What have you observed in your parents that you'd like to emulate when it comes to parenting or becoming empty nesters?
- What would you like to do in a different way than your parents did?
- Tell your spouse one thing you appreciate about their support during this season of your marriage.

Chapter Eight

IT'S ALL RELATIVE

We named our boys Dallas and Austin. There is no special meaning behind that decision other than we liked the names. If Austin had been a girl, I wanted to name him Alyssa Joy, using parts of both of our mother's names. But we knew weeks before he was born that he was a boy, or as the ultrasound tech put it, "You're going to be able to use those boy clothes again."

He came into the world with his dimpled cheeks face up. Momentarily, the doctor confirmed, "It's a boy." So, the name Alyssa went into the archives and our family was complete. After multiplying our family from two into four, life got into a groove and we sort of acted like this is how our family was going to look forever. We didn't always think about the idea that we might get

> Somehow Michelle wasn't thrilled with how I liked to wrestle with the boys in the living room. We would go until one of them accidentally elbowed me in the face and I got a nosebleed. Great memories. *—Phil*

bonus kids someday when our boys would choose a wife. Okay, to be honest, I thought about it often, since I'm the only girl and I so wanted someone to watch the Hallmark Channel with me in my pajamas. There is only so much a woman can handle of floor wrestling, Nerf guns, and dirt bikes. But I don't think Phil thought about it much.

In the summer after his graduation from high school, Austin started spending a lot of time with a girl we knew well from church. They went on a mission trip together, and shortly after, they were officially dating. They dated throughout college, got engaged, and a month after his college graduation he married—wait for it—Alyssa.

Alyssa Marie became our bonus daughter, and I discovered the fun of having a girl in the family. One year and a few months later, Dallas married Amy after a whirlwind year that followed a date set up by friends, and we gained another bonus daughter. Both are a wonderful addition to our family and well suited for our boys. Now, we are a family of six. And there's great news on the mother-in-law front! The girls watch Hallmark movies with me and eat chocolate.

We're looking forward to the day when we become Mimi and Papa, or Gigi and Gaga, or whatever. That will bring more bonuses into our family. What fun that will be!

As we think about bonus family members, some are biological, and others are added in through new connections. Let's declare all mother-in-law jokes forever banished; bonus is a privilege. It is something unexpected and special, an extra benefit.

> Adding two daughters-in-law to our family has given me the opportunity to have the daughters I never had. I get to reap the benefits of the good stuff! I didn't have to raise adolescent girls—thank goodness—but I get to appreciate the fun they bring to our family now. I'm thankful for *their* parents who raised girls who are kind and fun and who are polite enough to laugh when I try to be funny. *—Phil*

> Let's tell them! While we were writing this, we found out that the first grandbaby is on the way. *—Phil*

Biological Bonus Family

Let's talk a little about how family members can affect a marriage. When I married Phil, I had a lot to learn about family dynamics. We talked about family of origin in chapter 6. That has to do with how our past affects our present. Here we are going to focus on how family connections affect our future.

> Having two sets of parents means double the support. I have always felt love and support from both Michelle's parents and mine. I know that isn't the case for every couple, and I know it's a blessing to have parents who have your back. —*Phil*

First, our parents. My parents live independently and are quite active. So is Phil's dad. He rides a Harley motorcycle all over the US exploring by himself. But there will likely come a day when at least one of our parents will need help. Some couples reading this book have a parent living in their home. That parent might be fully independent or dependent on you for care. No matter the situation, there is a different dynamic when you have a parent in the house, similar to how it's different with children in the house.

Even if your parents don't share a roof with you, their well-being might be part of your responsibility—arranging care, supervising the living situation, or chauffeuring to appointments. As a couple, you will need to plan strategically for how you will not let your relationship waver.

Another part of our bonus family is extended family. When Phil's cousins first stayed with us for Christmas, I was wiped out. They are a fun-loving, boisterous bunch, and I love them all. But as a twenty-one-year-old newlywed, I wasn't prepared for the energy level in our little mobile home. Phil stepped up to give me a hand and made sure I held it together as the whole bunch of us maneuvered around the makeshift beds on the floor and took turns in the bathroom.

After everyone finished getting ready on the first morning, every towel we owned was dirty—even the wedding gift ones. We fried pounds of bacon and scrambled dozens of eggs in that weekend and kept our tiny washer and dryer earning their keep. What I have learned over the

> When my cousins and I get together, we like to play rowdy card games such as spoons or Uno, tear around on 4-wheelers and dirt bikes, and blow stuff up. With legal explosives. What did you think I meant? I think Michelle hit the jackpot with this Rayburn bonus family. *—Phil*

years is that along with their contagious but rowdy joy there is a loyal and caring love for family that I wouldn't trade or dull or diminish. Bonus family is, indeed, beautiful.

Both Phil and I have siblings, and our relationship with them has a big effect on our marriage as well. For all sorts of reasons, connecting with siblings as in-laws has its wonderful moments along with the struggles. Siblings share the same family traditions, and the spouse is the outsider.

It's easy to feel lonely or left out in a family gathering where the in-laws have inside jokes, stories that date back several decades to road trips, memories, gatherings, and tragedies. In our families we also have different ways of handling conflict. Think about how different your family is from your spouse's; some families hash it out, and others run away. Some families are blunt and bold; others much softer in what they say.

When we get married, we begin a life-long process of learning this about each other's families. Some of the lessons come hard and laced with sarcasm, and we're stretched to learn grace and keep our tongues muted. Along with that also comes the wonder of sharing a last name, experiencing love and acceptance, and becoming part of a legacy together. It's the most unusual mingling of cultures and tradition.

Bonus Family that Is Not Biological

Our daughters-in-law bring us much joy. They are wonderful, and I can't say enough about how much I appreciate their place in our family. But as a mother-in-law, I have to know my place. These girls didn't grow up in our family, and they don't know our expectations or unspoken rules. They come with their own sets of traditions and family boundaries.

They are all adults, meaning it isn't my job to parent our boys or their wives. If they cross my boundaries, I have to know how to be assertive without being bossy or harming relationships. Our desire is that they feel welcome in our family, but to also let our children know that Dad and I have our own relationship, and we need our space too. As our kids each work on their own marriages, we become the example. That's a lot of pressure! We might not always get it right. But we value grace, and we treasure relationships.

Let's look at some other non-biological family. If you're a blended family, you know you have some biological connections and some that are not. Blended doesn't really sound like a nice word, when you stop to think of it, because it sounds like losing your own identity. I believe

> I tell our boys often, "Learn from my mistakes, boys. Listen to your wife." –*Phil*

the intent behind the term is to encourage a harmony where everyone has their part, and they all get along. Maybe a "symphony" family would be a better term for a family of different biological origins who come together—some with mom, and some with dad—to form a new family.

I'm not talking an artificially perfect *The Brady Bunch* family here, but one where it's accepted to be yourself at the same time as you learn to appreciate the differences in others, and one where the connected biological families are celebrated rather than demonized.

Stepparents and stepsiblings don't always get along, and the biological parent is pulled in a lot of directions. Exes, who are biologically connected to the children, are sometimes friendly and sometimes hostile. You might need to see each other at school events, recitals, weddings—you know, the important stuff of life.

So, I acknowledge that it's complicated. I applaud those who have created a solid home, a strong marriage, and a stable emotional environment with their own symphony where a second marriage includes the bonus of children.

Divorce isn't the only reason for a second marriage. I've been researching my family tree lately, and I'm surprised to find out how common it was one hundred years ago for someone to lose a spouse at a young age. Several of my ancestors and one grandparent passed away in their sixties. That's a short life! Phil's grandma was a sister to his grandpa's first wife, who died when she was very young and left behind two children. That wasn't unusual then.

If your spouse was widowed before you were married, there is another person in your relationship who you will never meet. The memories and traditions from their marriage will add flavor to yours. It's up to you if you receive that as a sweet flavor or if it brings bitterness to you. That marriage might include bonus adult children who belong to your spouse; they have lost a mother or a father and need space to grieve.

Someone who falls in love with a person who is widowed might think jealously or resentment for the first spouse will never cross their minds. But in real life, we're all human. It will be challenging to leave space for bonus kids to remember their parent, especially if the sharing of memories leaves the new spouse feeling on the outside of the conversation.

Rules for Survival

> Rules make me feel as if I'm in school. Will there be a quiz on this? *–Phil*

I like rules. This is kind of a problem, since rules rarely lead to much good. Let's look at these not as legalistic hammer-and-gavel law sort of rules but more like some guidelines for how we can pledge to make our marriage relationship a priority—with some grace blended in too. These "rules" are commitments we make to each other regarding bonus family members.

Rule number one: Your marriage comes above all other relationships. If you've been divorced and are already living with divorce guilt, boot that out of your mind and put that energy into your new marriage. If you have children who have been through a divorce with you, let them experience the stability that comes from living with spouses who put each other above the kids, conflict, pets, and projects. Your marriage comes above your parents, siblings, in-laws, and even your darling little grandbabies.

Rule number two: See rule number one.

> That was much better than I thought. *–Phil*

Easy peasy lemon squeezy, right? Oh, who am I kidding? Of course it's going to be difficult to do that! So, we need some rules for our rule. Policies. Boundaries. Principles. Parameters. Whatever you want to call them, we need to plan ahead if we are going to keep our marriage a priority. These are some ideas that have worked for us:

- **Establish boundaries.** Talk about how you will create boundaries. How will you make decisions? How will you say no? What will you say if one of *your* family members steps over the boundary and hurts your spouse? What if your spouse's family puts pressure on your relationship? Establish boundaries regarding how much time you will spend with other family, especially your parents. How much will you depend on family for childcare, money, advice, or assistance? These are all easier to navigate when you have boundaries set before it comes to a conflict.

- **Keep your emotions in check.** Someone is going to say something hurtful at some time, or you are not a human family. I get a D plus at keeping my emotions in check. Maybe I've improved to a C minus now that I'm a mature fifty-year-old. I'm practicing and getting better. How will you respond? How will you show grace? What will you do if your feelings get hurt? Having a plan helps in the heat of the moment. You may have to remind yourself often to not take things personally.

- **Say positive things about your spouse in front of other relatives.** Build each other up and talk about how proud you are of each other. If your relatives hear the great stuff about your spouse, they will have a much better opinion of them, which will also make life easier for both of you.

- **Commit to not complain to other relatives about each other.** Why share with your mother about your disappointment with your husband? Talk it out with him. The exception to this is when you're in an abusive situation or you are not safe. Scrap these rules and reach out, then. Please! But in a typical healthy marriage where you strive to improve in communication, the first boundary starts with working things out between the two of you first.

- **Don't put each other in a position to choose sides.** I'll admit there were times when I challenged my husband to choose his mother or me. He wanted us both happy, but that wasn't possible. I know that wasn't fair to him. Don't make him choose between you or his children, or you or his parents. Instead, work together to find a resolution that honors your relationship without destroying the other relationships in your life.

- **Agree to stand up for each other.** The best thing you can do for your marriage is to let your spouse know you have their back, that they are your number one, and that you will defend them from wounds from your own family. That is a big challenge, but an important commitment. There have been times when I have longed for Phil to stand up and say, "Hey, that's my wife you're talking about." He is a middle child and a peacekeeper, so this is difficult for him. A few times when our teenage boys tested me, he stepped in to say, "Don't speak to your mother that way." I appreciated that so much!

> I hardly ever love it when Michelle is direct with me about when I have done something that upsets her, but I am thankful that she talks about it with me and doesn't complain to her mom. We work it out, even if conflict isn't fun. That way, her parents still like me too. —*Phil*

When you've been married long enough, biological and bonus all start to run together. Phil treats my parents just like his own. I don't remember when I started calling his parents mom and dad, but I did. Eventually, we realize that family is family. It doesn't matter if we are born there or are transplanted and grafted in later; we love each other anyway.

Phil and I have been part of each other's families for longer than the solo time we were part of our own nuclear families. Wow! The longer we are away, the more solid the glue becomes in our bond as a couple. I believe it takes a lifetime for the two to become one. When the two moms light candles before the ceremony on the wedding day of their children and then the bride and groom light their unity candle shortly after, this is only a symbol of who they promise to become; it is not who they immediately are.

We promise to forsake all others. We promise to make our union a priority. We promise to love and cherish. But in reality, it takes practice to live that out. Marriage is a process of learning and becoming. As if putting two imperfect humans into a lifetime commitment to

> I don't talk up Michelle's strengths in front of in-laws and bonus family as much as I could. Brag about your spouse when you can! –*Phil*

love each other isn't enough of a challenge, God apparently has a sense of humor, and he offers us some bonus people to make sure we have opportunities to prove we really mean it. He also uses those same people to be an incredible source of blessing and encouragement. Go God! That's pretty creative.

There's a verse in the Bible that sums up a goal we can aspire to in our family relationships:

> Let your conversation be gracious and attractive so that you will have the right response for everyone. (Colossians 4:6)

Tune-Up Time

For each of the following, say whether you agree or disagree, and then discuss why you agree or disagree with the statement. Listen to one another and try to understand your spouse's point of view.

Agree or disagree:

- I feel respected by the bonus family in our life (children, in-laws, exes, siblings).
- I think our families cause friction between us.
- We have clear boundaries when it comes to making our relationship the top priority.
- I have told my family members how proud I am of my spouse.
- I think we are growing in our unity with one another.
- For parents of married children—We do well with showing love and support for the spouses of our children as they incorporate into our family.
- For "symphony" families—We have created a loving and peaceful home where all of our children feel appreciated and accepted.

As you continue your discussion, review the rule in this chapter: your marriage comes above all other relationships.

- On a scale of 1–10, with ten being the highest, how do you rate your commitment to doing this? (You might not have the same number. Talk about how one of you might feel much more positive about this than the other does.)

- Discuss at least one of the following steps you can take to establish a principle that will help to prioritize your marriage:

    * Establish boundaries.
    * Keep your emotions in check.
    * Say positive things about your spouse in front of other relatives.
    * Commit to not complain to other relatives about each other.
    * Don't put each other in a position to choose sides.
    * Agree to stand up for each other.

- Establish a time in about month or so where you can talk about this step and evaluate how you're doing.
- Take a few minutes to pray together to thank God for the bonus family he has given you and ask him to teach you how to have gracious conversations and healthy interaction with family.

Fun

Chapter Nine

TRADING HOBBIES

"*Honey, I shot a buck,*" I announced as I trudged in the back door in my oversized blaze orange get-up. "I'll need you to come out and gut him for me."

"How many points?" he asked as he set down a laundry basket.

"Six," I answered. "Only one shot."

"Good for you! I'll help after dinner."

My rosy cheeks confirmed my six hours in a deer stand, and his lack of the usual drip on the end of his nose suggested he had been warming in the house for quite some time.

"You're doing laundry?" Something was very backwards in this picture.

"Got cold out there."

❧

I can't say that I've ever been a big fan of the outdoors, even though I grew up on a dairy farm. I usually preferred the inside chores or gardening, and neat and tidy hobbies like sewing, crochet, and of course, shopping.

I hate bugs. I don't like getting my hair messed up. And I don't like any kind of camping that doesn't involve electricity, hot showers, hair dryers, curling irons, or air mattresses. I am not earthy. I am wimpy.

I had always envisioned myself with at least one little girl. I dreamed I would brush her hair and put little pink bows in it. We would paint our toenails. We'd go shopping. We'd talk about boys and have slumber parties. But then, I gave birth to two boys and I became the only woman in a three-man household.

Taking it Back

I recall more than a few times in our marriage when I have ridiculed Phil's passion for spending hours confined to a bucket-sized platform at the top of a tree-clinging ladder. "What's the point of freezing yourself up there without bringing meat home?" I have mocked.

> I have always loved the peace and quiet of the woods after a long day of work. But there were times when it frustrated Michelle to have me head out there after she had already spent a long day with the kids. —*Phil*

But sometimes he did bring meat home. And I had to learn how to cook wild game so it would taste like a juicy beef steak. When I learned to cook, I never learned how to cook a deer. Certainly, I never dreamed I'd serve grilled deer for company. But I did. Well, in the civilized world, they call it venison. But it's really grilled deer.

Because of my lack of fish and game aptitude, mocking hunting videos used to be one of my hobbies. I was merciless. Phil would pop one in for evening entertainment—imagine videos before Netflix and Hulu ruled the world—and I'd start thinking of ways I could ridicule the men on the video. I mean, really, it seemed more like comedy to watch grown men choke with emotion and clutch their erratically beating hearts at the sight of antlers. The cameraman would zoom in on a

> Sometimes a man can't watch another man shoot the buck of a lifetime without his wife making fun of the whole process. How is this any different from the women who cry their eyes out when they "say yes to the dress"? —*Phil*

wild-eyed hunter as he whispered in a raspy voice about the buck that had wandered under the stand, and I'd fall over in spasms of laughter.

But as my boys grew older and they started doing stuff with my husband, I longed for ways to connect with the three of them. They weren't interested in painting toenails or styling our hair. When I found out my hairdresser was a deer hunter, I sputtered, "But, you're so . . . feminine!" Her revelation made me think it was time to discover exactly what it was that drew my husband to the outdoors.

> She probably wouldn't find it so funny if she knew how much money they got paid to film those hunting videos. Too late for a new career? —*Phil*

I told Phil I was going to try his hobbies.

We tried fishing. The first time, he looked me up and down and said, "You're wearing make-up."

"Is that a crime?"

"We're fishing, you know."

I knew. What did it hurt to look pretty while I batted my lashes at him asking for yet another worm on my hook?

It was endearing to sit in the boat with Phil away from the television and other distractions. We talked. He was so sweet about taking the fish off for me and putting creepy bait on my hook. I felt closer to him.

> I prefer leeches. But she wouldn't get in the boat with them. —*Phil*

When I suggested that I try deer hunting, he tilted one eyebrow. Then he took me shopping for blaze orange.

Phil's preparation for a morning of hunting includes a shower with special scent-masking soap. He airs his hunting clothes outside for weeks and sprays everything with a foul liquid that makes him smell like dirt and rotten apples. On the other hand, I jammed my hair-sprayed tresses under a fluorescent cap with no worry about the cologne lingering on my sweatshirt. He suggested we hunt from different stands.

> There is a fine art to this process. The deer cannot know that a human is in the woods. —*Phil*

I was okay with that. I asked my daddy to sit with me, and he was happy to comply.

Within hours of sitting in the woods, I knew exactly why Phil loves it. In the hush of the breeze in the treetops and the squirrels stirring leaves, I could escape with my thoughts. The telephone didn't ring. No one hollered, "Mom, where do we keep the plunger?" The only interruption to the solitude was my dad snoring in the seat next to me. I figured he'd snap awake if I shot anything.

At the first sight of a deer, my legs shook as they did when I gave birth to our first son. My heart pounded and I took back every word of previous ridicule. "What is wrong with me?" I thought. "I'm losing all credibility as a hunting scoffer."

> Did my wife just say she was wrong? I'm glad we got that in print. —*Phil*

When a six-point buck walked by my stand, I raised my rifle. It's a lot harder without the Pepsi logo to shoot at. Pop cans also don't move. This was real hunting.

I aimed where Phil had taught me to point the scope.

At the crack of the rifle, the deer leaped in the air and then took off into the woods.

"Missed," I said to my dad. My legs were numb from the knees down.

I could hear the deer crashing through nearby brush. We waited a few minutes until the woods quieted and I could stand on my jelly legs, then my dad said, "Let's go for a little walk."

Not far from where I'd seen the back side of the deer disappear into the underbrush, there was my buck.

"One shot! You dropped him with one shot." I could hear the pride in my dad's voice. "Let's go get some lunch and see if we can find Phil to help us."

> I'm proud of her. She's always been a better shot at target practice, so it didn't surprise me. It isn't like she took up hunting as a life-long sport, but she did it for a few years. The best outcome of the experience was that she learned what I loved so much about hunting. There is nothing like a peaceful tree stand after a hard day of work. —*Phil*

I couldn't wait to tell him all about my talents as a hunter. I couldn't wait to apologize for years of tormenting him either. I never thought I'd ever grill a deer that I had shot myself.

Returning the Favor

This hobby trading isn't one-sided. Phil has reciprocated. I had the same sense of closeness to him the first time he sat at the table with me and rubber stamped a greeting card. He's probably hoping I changed his name on this book so his buddies won't question his testosterone balance. I'm sure he'd rather they didn't know that he sometimes sneaks down to my craft stash to create hand-made cards for my birthday and other holidays—to the envy of my girlfriends.

My excitement over finding the perfect slacks on sale at the mall is equal to his excitement over bagging a ten-point buck. He has shown patience on more than one mall bench while I bag a trophy bargain. I guess I can return the favor by welcoming another head-mount for the wall.

> No. You didn't just tell people this. —*Phil*

Making It Work

Which of your spouse's hobbies makes you roll your eyes and sigh? Perhaps you have mocked her love of sappy chick flicks or resented his passion for eighteen holes of golf.

Trying one another's hobbies has enriched our marriage. Since I experienced Phil's thrill for hunting, I complain less about the time he spends in the woods. Since he understands the joy I receive from crafting, he doesn't fret about the cost of paper and supplies. Seeing through the other's eyes has given us a new appreciation for each other.

A second benefit of swapping hobbies is the bond that comes from spending time together. We laugh with each other. We laugh at each other—in a healthy way. We create lasting memories as we learn from one another, and it keeps us from living separate lives. Besides, it's a cheap way of dating.

Finally, trying one another's hobbies is a sacrificial act. If Phil has no

> We colored together on one date night. She promised not to put that on social media. Turns out, I can color inside the lines. Go figure! It was actually more fun than I want to admit. —*Phil*

interest in going to a piano concert, it is an act of sacrifice for him to commit not only to going but also to being tolerant and not ridiculing my interest in that art.

I have no desire to humiliate myself on the golf course, but if Phil asked, I could sacrifice enough pride to hit a few balls at the driving range with him during off-peak hours. It takes some creativity to find ways to make it work, and it takes a sacrificial attitude to let go of personal preference, but occasionally trading hobbies can be a marriage-enriching adventure.

I'll admit, my attitude wasn't so great when I tried Boundary Waters canoeing for a day with Phil. For just a day, though, because I wasn't brave enough to do a whole week like he does. And I didn't think he could tolerate my whining for that long anyway. We were camping at a state park in northern Minnesota and decided to trailer the canoe to the landing point where he begins his Boundary Waters trips, and we paddled around for a few hours.

I wasn't as successful at embracing that hobby. My attitude went south as we paddled north. The bugs, the portaging of the gear, the lack of bathrooms and electricity—it didn't thrill me. At least I tried it. He won't be taking up knitting any day between now and eternity either.

We will continue to be open-minded about the hobbies we each enjoy. I'm just thankful he isn't into hang gliding.

> I guess Michelle agreed with my cousin Rick, who said that portaging a bunch of camping and fishing gear across a strip of land between two lakes is equal to disassembling a Chevy truck, transporting the parts in multiple two-mile trips, then reassembling it. —*Phil*

Ode to Rifle Season
by Michelle Rayburn

'Tis the night before hunting and all through the house
Each rifle's been polished by kinner and spouse
They've laid out the blaze orange and boots by the door
With plans to be up by 5:30 fo' sho'
They'll climb in a tree stand somewhere before dawn
But likely the first thing they'll see is a fawn
Then later mid-morning awaken mid-nap
To the sight of a trophy and mutter, "O snap!"
Raising the rifle not making a sound
The hunter will drop that big buck to the ground
He'll drag the thing home, hang it up in a tree
And ask his poor wife to come look and see
She'll give him the requisite "oo" and "ah"
Then say, "That's great honey! I had fun at the spa."

Ode to Shopping

Roses are red,
violets are blue,
I'll pay to get out of
shopping with you.

–Phil

Tune-Up Time

- Which of your spouse's hobbies have you not tried but would be willing to try?
- Talk about which of your spouse's hobbies you have resented or made fun of.
- Think back in your experiences together and name some activities one of you did just to make the other person happy. What did you learn about each other in that experience?
- Come up with a list of ideas you could try as a couple's activity, even if only one of you is passionate about it.
- What is your most treasured memory of something you did together?
- Without help from your partner, name what you think his or her favorite hobby is.
- Let's practice appreciating things through our spouse's eyes. Explain what you think your partner loves about their favorite hobby.
  * What emotions does it produce in them?
  * How does it validate their interests?
  * What special skills do they use in this hobby?
  * What awards or accomplishments have they received in this activity?

Chapter Ten

PASSIONATE SHEET MUSIC

"*I'm not in the mood.*" Five little words that spell death to desire. I know some of you guys skipped straight to this chapter. And you want to read the whole thing, not just Phil's comments. I get it. This is your favorite topic in the whole book. It was Phil's favorite topic when we participated in an eight-week marriage course at church. I want you to understand it's important to your wife too. It might be a little more complicated for her, but it's still important.

When one spouse says, "I'm not in the mood," it's as if it isn't spoken in English. By this, I mean, it's as if those words have hidden meaning that translate into something else when it crosses from one spouse's lips, floats through the tense air, and lands on the ears of the other spouse. What he or she hears might be something more like this:

"I'm repulsed by you."

"You're ugly."

"I don't love you."

"We will never have sex again. Ever."

We may as well play a Taylor Swift song about never ever, ever getting back together.

What that phrase really means is, "I'm not in the mood right now." That's it. You see the pronoun in that line? For those who hated English class and diagramming sentences, here is a clue: I is a pronoun. It is first person, meaning it is about me. It means there is something within me that is affecting my mood. It also means it isn't your job to get me in the mood, and it isn't about you (more pronouns). Well, I understand it's about you in that you were hoping for some fun, and right now it isn't happening. But let's take a deep breath and set aside what each of us wants and find a common ground somewhere.

> Frankly, I'm speechless. I want to create special editions of the book for our kids and family with this chapter removed. Just kidding. Not kidding. –*Phil*

Intimacy is important in a marriage. If you have kids in the room right now, we're talking about s-e-x. If you have a husband in the room, he's reading over your shoulder, because he saw the first page of the chapter and wondered what that was all about. If you're a husband reading, we're talking about how to make sure your number one need is met. You're welcome.

This is probably the most difficult chapter of this book for me to write. First, because it involves being vulnerable and talking about parts of our life that I don't discuss with other people—other than my husband. Second, because it's an area in our marriage that I'm still working on. Well, we're still working on, but I say I'm working on it because it's pretty simple for Phil. I give the sign, he says, "Really?" and there we go. But if he gives the sign, I have a whole list of considerations that I need to process. If your relationship looks a lot like this, then stick around; I'll have something to say to each of you.

The third reason for why this is a difficult chapter to write is that my parents might read this book. Our children and their wives might read it. This is not something we sit around discussing over Easter dinner. I hope that in the end it will help them to understand we're human. Don't

Sex and Sleep are Not the Same

Why in the world do we refer to sex as sleeping together? Sleep is what happens when our exhausted bodies fall into bed and we race to see who can fall

> Cover your ears kids.
> –*Phil*

asleep first so that we don't have to listen to the other person snore. It's about winding down our heart rate and paying no attention to the person beside us. Sex is quite the opposite. The only thing they have in common is that they usually take place in the same room. Okay two things. Both are typically horizontal.

Gals, if your husband said, "Sweetie, I'd like to sleep with you," wouldn't you take him up on the offer?

You'd brush your teeth, take out your contacts, hop into the saggy sweats you've owned since college, and climb into bed.

I suspect that the first person who said someone "slept" together did it with air quotes—like what I just did here. Perhaps it was used in a sentence such as this: "Connie said she was too tired to go home after the party last night, so she and Darryl 'slept' together in his room." Wink.

Speaking of phrases we use, who came up with making love? Sex does not manufacture love. It is an expression of love. It is the act of giving your body to the person you love and wholly trusting them. But if a woman thinks having sex with her boyfriend is going to manufacture love that isn't there, she's likely going to end up with a broken heart. This is why sex outside of marriage is a challenge.

In chapter 16, we'll talk about why the covenant of marriage is important in the physical relationship too. But for now, let's focus on the physical and emotional connection that sexual intimacy offers. If these were out of order in your relationship—you had sex before your marriage—my goal is not to shame you. If you had other partners before your marriage, my goal is not to condemn you. What we practice doesn't always line up with God's best plan, but he can redeem it, even when we take a turn down a path that leads to a struggle.

I would also like to mention that many men think physical touch is their love language, based on the five love languages outlined by author Gary Chapman.[4] But when we did the love languages assessment it confirmed what I thought; Phil's primary love language is words of affirmation, and his second is acts of service.

Because men desire sex and it is an innate need, they believe it is their love language. For some, it is. In my observation, they are the ones who touch everybody they meet in nonsexual ways. They touch your shoulder when you're speaking to them and pat your back as you

> Learning this about myself was a surprise to me too. –*Phil*

walk away. They also tend to get in your personal space when they're talking—you know, like they cross the no-zone and get way too close to your nose. But for some people, it is only sexual touch that they desire. This isn't the same.

It's important for sure. But if we know what makes our spouse feel loved and appreciated (their love language), and we combine that with sexual intimacy, then we have a recipe for a strong relationship!

Once Upon a Time

Let's go back to the beginning of your relationship. Perhaps you remember a time when you could barely keep your hands off each other. Maybe that was this morning. But if you can't remember when that was, then this is for you.

Remember your dating days and counting down to having sex? For those of us who waited until marriage for this, there was a lot of anticipation leading up to the wedding day. Even if you didn't wait, there was a point where your relationship crossed into a physical one. And I'm guessing it happened with frequency at first.

Maybe it wasn't what you expected. Or maybe the experience fulfilled all of your dreams. Perhaps physical limitations have made your own sexual expression different from someone else's. As a couple, we each develop our own version of intimacy and expression of love for our spouse. The movies make it look so perfect, but real life makes that look like a joke.

Over time, it's likely something changed in your relationship. You got too busy, too tired, too pregnant, or too overwhelmed. If all these "toos" have led to sex being too infrequent, it might be time for a reset. If a husband is still reading over the shoulder, he may be nodding at this moment.

Start with Communication

Our biggest struggle has been with how to communicate about intimacy. How to send the right messages, how to express our own frustrations. I want to put this out there because I have heard other women say it, too. This is the chain of events that happens too often: the wife wants their relationship to include tender, nonsexual touch, so she accepts a pat on the behind from her husband and a playful kiss. It makes her feel loved and appreciated. He gives her a little shoulder rub and she thinks, "This is nice." But then the hands start to move under her blouse, and she realizes it's going a little further than she anticipated. She puts an end to the moment because now her husband is clearly indicating he wants sex.

> We're not sex therapists or experts. Make sure people know that. —*Phil*

But that isn't on her mind right now. She wants tenderness and understanding. Now he is frustrated. He gets angry and sulks away. In defense of his actions, let's acknowledge that he has physical needs. His timing is just off. Really off. Whether it is true or not, she eventually believes that he is only tender when he wants sex. She would like him to be affectionate for no reason at all. She feels insecure. He feels unloved. She decides that if all touch is going to lead to this constant battle, she isn't going to let it begin unless she's in the mood.

Here's the problem with that progression. Now, the only time she gets touch is when sex is involved. And she starts to feel as if her husband has an ulterior motive. He will be nice when he might get sex. But he will be a jerk if he doesn't. He might think there is a magical formula because of what worked in the past: he did the dishes, put the kids to bed, rubbed her feet, and they had sex.

If he thinks doing the dishes or folding the laundry will make himself appealing to her, he tries this. Or he tries the same "formula" as the last time. But then if that leads to a dead end, he's back to acting like a jerk. And she thinks if she's the least bit nice to him, he's going to assume she has romantic feelings toward him ... which sometimes leads right to a dead end.

> I've blown it in this area a lot of times. When I was young, I reacted in a way that totally didn't make things better. If you think getting angry at your spouse for not meeting your physical needs will make it better, think again. A cold shoulder won't either. Turning over and facing the wall, the silent treatment, sulking - nope, nope, nope. —*Phil*

And so, a wall goes up. She silently struggles with her body image and wanting to be cherished. He struggles with wondering why she never wants to touch him and why sex is always at the bottom of her list—why he is at the bottom of her list.

I know this doesn't happen in all relationships. But it is what happened in ours. Phil started to assume I hated all physical touch. And I figured everything nice that he did had an ulterior motive. He might admit he sometimes did have another motive. In the middle of that, I felt as if I had failed as a wife.

Guys, let me say this to be clear. There is no formula. Your wife is way more complicated than that.

How do we break this ugly cycle of rejection? Some of my dearest friends might say it's the wife's duty to fulfill her husband's physical needs. It's biblical that we should surrender our bodies to each other, but I have a hard time believing it means to lie there and wait for it to be over. But if she feels used and doesn't find any pleasure in sex—and I have met friends who have said they lived this scenario too—then a piece is still missing. It can be satisfying and fulfilling for both of you.

This might be too much information, but I have never "faked it" in my relationship with my husband. It has taken tears, arguments, sacrifice, and communication to get to where we are now, but frequency doesn't always indicate a healthy relationship. What makes it healthy is figuring out how to value your spouse. The angry and sullen standoffs in our relationship are gone. And I enjoy a tender hug from my husband at any

I don't want my wife to feel pressured, but I want her to know my needs. Figuring out how to communicate them without selfish motives is a learning process for me. I want her to feel loved and valued just as much. –*Phil*

time because they don't have strings attached. Where we had a season of discord, our relationship is harmonious. Getting here wasn't easy, but I'm so glad we got here.

Figure Out What Works for You

We've had to talk through my emotional barriers. I've reassured Phil that I was not repulsed by his presence. And we developed some signals—a note on the bathroom mirror, a text message, a note on the pillow. We've even practiced non-sexual affection. Really! It sounds robotic, but if you preface contact with a clear statement from either spouse, it's amazing how nice a warm hug is. Or a tender kiss. Or a shoulder rub. Or yes, even a swat on the backside while doing dishes.

"Permission to approach your personal space without strings attached."

"Permission granted."

Okay. It doesn't go like that. But if ridiculously awkward works for you, go for it!

What works for you will change in different seasons. Having teenagers in the house makes it difficult to have any sort of conversation—about money, conflict with a friend, or possible career changes—much less, one about sex! A weekend away might be the most privacy you'll ever get. Until the kids leave home. (Sorry kids if you're reading this.) This is when many couples rekindle their honeymoon phase and discover they are still best friends and great lovers.

As difficult as it is to communicate about this, talk with each other about any barriers you have in your physical relationship. I wish we had communicated and come to an understanding earlier in our marriage, but maybe neither of us was mature enough back then. Be more mature than we were and try to see it from your partner's perspective. –*Phil*

We don't sleep in the same room anymore. I just heard you gasp.

Is that judgment in your eyes? I have always wondered why it is that few people keep the ancient tradition of the royals and have their own bedchambers. But when our children left home, we discussed the idea of taking our own bedrooms. Stay with me here!

> Now we can do "sleep"-overs at each other's places sometimes. I do sleep better now that I have my own space. But we have to be intentional about making sure we don't become friends *without* benefits. *—Phil*

We spent so much of every night jabbing each other because of snoring. I tried ear plugs, and then got an ear infection. I tried noise machines and sleeping on my side. I tried a headband with speakers in it. Nothing worked. We are restless sleepers. I can't cuddle and sleep, and that was never part of our habit. I didn't feel more affectionate toward Phil by lying sleepless at night listening to him snort—yes, that's what he does. He didn't appreciate hearing me buzz away after his prostate would wake him up at 4:30, and the trip to the bathroom left him wide awake on his side of the bed.

So, we made an agreement that we would sleep in our own rooms, but still make time for intimacy. The deal was that it wasn't to separate us for anything but sleep. Now that we are both more rested, we like each other more. We sleep with very different room temperatures, which we also enjoy. We get up at different times and don't disturb each other. Sometimes I'll stop in his room in the morning to say hello and talk about our day.

This doesn't work for everyone, but it works for us. This is why I emphasize: figure out what works for you. And don't think poorly of someone if their choice is different from yours. If sleeping in different rooms would do nothing but put up a physical barrier for romance, then it isn't for you. Which leads us to the next point.

Navigate Physical Barriers

For a twenty-five-year-old, it might be impossible to imagine any physical change that would make sex more of a challenge, but as we age, we change.

Childbirth changes a woman's body. After she expands and deflates a couple of times, her belly and breasts might look a bit like a birthday balloon after most of the air has gone out of it—you know, the ones that fall behind the TV cabinet after they've lost all of their helium. Her breasts might point east and west when she lies on her back. She might be ashamed of how she looks in lingerie. She might want the lights off when he wants them on. As she goes through menopause, she might experience a wild spectrum of desire—from sex several times per week to, "When was the last time we did it?"

> Would your relationship hold together if there was a physical or medical reason for why you could not express yourselves sexually as you once did? Sex can't be the only thing that keeps you together. –*Phil*

Men aren't exempt either. Years of eating potato chips sort of does bad things to the blood pressure, which leads to prescription pills, which can contribute to erectile dysfunction. Testosterone starts to diminish. The prostate gets enlarged and contributes to issues. His desire might decrease. A couple might face the opposite of what they did two decades prior. Now it might be the husband who is struggling with his self-image about performance.

Again, communication is key. No shaming. Just honest talk about physical symptoms and feelings about it. Patiently help each other without pressing your own needs.

> Communication helps on both sides of a relationship. If you're the one who sends confusing signals and it isn't clear if you're "in the mood" when you flirt a little or give some affection, be direct and tell your partner this might go somewhere. Basically, "You wanna get lucky?" would work. We're going to leave this in the book, right? –*Phil*

Health crises might put a pause on your sexual expression. A crisis pregnancy that involves premature labor and bedrest means abstinence for a while. Cancer treatment, surgery, prostate removal, or a mastectomy for breast cancer bring major changes to your relationship. These are the types of situations we made promises about when we said, "In good times and in bad times, in sickness and in health." A lack of sex in our marriage for one of these reasons is not a license to have an affair. Well, there is never any license to have an affair—let's make that clear.

When a crisis comes, we turn inward toward each other for love and support. We bring God into our needs, but we don't seek outside of our marriage for what we don't have within it.

Minimize Distractions

Once I made a reservation at a nice hotel that was twenty minutes from our home. I drove there during the afternoon to check in and drop off our overnight bags, then went back home to wait for Phil to get off work. He thought we were simply going out to dinner at the hotel, but after we finished eating, I asked him if he'd like to go upstairs. He gave me a funny look and then I flashed the key to a room.

Sometimes, we need to get away from home and minimize distractions. For me dishes are a distraction. Clutter and laundry are distractions. To-do lists are a distraction. For some it is cell phones or television shows that keep us from paying attention to each other. Or hobbies. Or work. Whatever it is, it's important to make time for each other.

> Hey, some of the best dates are to a home improvement store. They even sell chocolate there. And flowers. And they have that fresh lumber smell. –*Phil*

We've learned that driving thirty minutes to go out to dinner in a noisy restaurant isn't always relaxing. We don't have the best conversations there. And it usually means stopping at the home improvement store or the grocery store—neither of which are romantic. We've found that we can enjoy a much more intimate conversation at home with Pandora playing music while we put a puzzle together. We turn off our cell phones and pay attention to each other. A date night doesn't always have to end with sex, but we make sure we connect at the heart level.

Protect Your Marriage

No one else is going to protect your marriage like you can. This means it is up to you to protect the sacredness of what the Bible calls your "marriage bed." If lust is a problem, address how you will lust-proof your marriage.

If you're drawn to trashy shows, remove them from your lineup of favorites. They do nothing to enhance your intimacy. There is nothing that turns me off more than having Phil scroll through the channels and hesitate at some show that is all about how "sex sent me to the ER" or something like that. Along with explicit shows, pornography has no place in a marriage. Someone reading this is going to advocate for "to each his own" or say that it helps get them in the mood. Having another couple in your bedroom, even if on a screen, does not help your marriage in the long run. There are plenty of studies and statistics to prove it too.

Real connection with each other is the way to get yourself in the mood. To my women friends, this is for you too. Books about fifty shades of erotica are not helpful to your marriage. Neither are trashy romance novels. They aren't just innocent entertainment. They get into your brain and speak messages when you least expect them.

In addition to boundaries about media, it's important to establish boundaries about friends of the opposite gender and about conduct on business trips for work. Seriously. You aren't a prude for doing this. Every boundary you set up adds security to your marriage and bonds you closer to each other. I've already mentioned I don't meet with men for lunch or travel to a conference alone together. I'm even careful about who I friend on social media if I think they'll try to push my boundaries.

❧

Now that I've crossed over the TMI threshold, I hope you can learn from our vulnerability. Work on it together and talk it out. If you're in a sexless marriage, are you willing to take the first steps toward each other again? Will you begin with conversation? When there is harmony in the bedroom, it does bring a beautiful melody into the other parts of our relationship. Our prayer for you is that together you will experience beautiful and passionate sheet music.

> Okay, kids. You can uncover your ears again. —*Phil*

Tune-Up Time

This could be an interesting conversation to have in a restaurant. This would also be a perfect date night to have in a private place, on a getaway, or for a stay-home date too. Privacy allows you the comfort to talk openly without inhibition. Discuss whether or not you agree with the following statements and why:

- I am satisfied with our current frequency of lovemaking.
- I feel as if my sexual needs are fulfilled.
- I feel comfortable with my body.
- We are more emotionally intimate than ever before.

More questions for discussion:

- Describe the first time you kissed each other.
- On a scale of 0–10 with ten being the highest, how important is non-sexual touch and affection to you in your relationship? (Holding hands, hugging, sitting close, etc.)
- When you engage in non-sexual touch or affection with each other, what does that communicate to you?
- What are some of your biggest obstacles when it comes to sex?
- What kills the mood for you like nothing else?
- What turns you on more than anything else?

Chapter Eleven

SOLE MATES FOR LIFE

An editor or English teacher probably just flipped out and choked on a piece of chocolate while reading the title of this chapter. Breathe. This is not a typo. Phil hated homonyms in school, so when writers like me get clever and play with words, it messes with his brain. It's no wonder he can't remember which two, to, or too he should use. Is it a sneak peek or a sneak peak? Is this their coffee they're leaving over there to cool off? You see how confusing it is? Let me explain why I felt this cleverness with words was so important.

I don't think we find our soul mates; I think we become them by being sole mates. With this definition, sole mates are two people who may or may not believe they were destined from

> Michelle has a way with words, and sometimes the clever stuff goes over my head–like homonyms. I hate those things. Interesting that I have a son who is an English teacher and a wife who is a writer. Glad they love that stuff. *–Phil*

the beginning of time to be together, but who are committed only—solely—to each other, no matter what comes.

Love at First Sight?

I met Phil when I was fifteen years old and we started dating the summer I turned sixteen. We were young and immature, but our relationship is more than three decades old. How did I know my husband was the right one for me? I didn't know from the moment our eyes locked across the church sanctuary. Nor was it love at first date. Yet, at some point I knew he was the one for me.

I ran across a blog post once in which the author declared that her husband is not her soul mate. The author's observations about marriage and the daily commitment it takes were precisely right. But the concept of a "soul mate" captured my thoughts. I disagreed with her idea that we couldn't be connected at the soul level with our spouse. But I also disagree with the idea others have presented, saying we need to roam the world until we discover the one person uniquely put on earth only for us.

Here is how it's often perceived to work: a girl makes a list

> I first laid eyes on Michelle from across the church sanctuary when her family visited our church. I'll be honest, I thought she was ten or twelve, so there was no love at first sight. However, when my mother introduced us after the service and asked me to take her to Sunday School, I realized she was a fellow high schooler. Now that she's in her 50s, she isn't disappointed when people think she's in her 30s. But I got off track there like a Jeep out of alignment. I was talking about thinking she was cute, but too young for me.
> —*Phil*

of the qualities she wants in a husband, she waits because God has this one man picked out for her, and when they find each other, they'll live happily ever after. Translated: she must search until she finds that one person God chose for her. The heavens will part, and her heart will flutter when she finally meets that man. She will know in the depths of her soul that God has written their future in the stars, or something like that.

What's wrong with this? It sets up a fairy tale with expectations potentially too high for any human to reach. And there is no biblical support for the concept as defined this way. The idea of a list of characteristics that the perfect mate will have is also flawed if we have created such a list without consulting God about it. There is no biblical indication that God will bend his will to meet mine. Rather, it's the other way around.

> I wasn't looking for a soul mate at eighteen years old. I was actually looking for a Honda XL350R (dirt bike, for those not familiar with it) to come into my life. And I was a bit surprised when this girl suddenly had me thinking about combing my hair and eating breath mints. Showering was suddenly a part of my daily routine.
> —*Phil*

I won't throw away the idea of a soul mate. But I have redefined it. The problem is with how we're misguided in our definition of the term. I believe my husband is my soul mate because we are sole mates.

I believe in God's sovereignty, and I believe he will lead me to make decisions that are in my best interest if I keep my heart surrendered to his leading. I believe that when two people keep their hearts in tune with God, he will lead them to a mate who complements each. When God is in charge of a marriage, two people become sole mates because their souls are each so tied to God that they become one with each other.

Perhaps, rather than being a mate chosen for me from the beginning of time, my husband is a godly man who crossed my path at a time when we were both open to God's leading in our lives and ready to surrender to that path together. And the list of qualities I'd dream of in a husband? Godly and loving were the only two items that needed to remain on the list. The rest were artificial "needs." When God brought Phil into my life, he didn't have many of the traits on my wish list, yet I knew he was right for me.

We have chosen to love only each other for the rest of our days, or until death changes that. God does have a plan for every person's life. For some, it is to marry. For others it isn't. For those who marry, it is impossible to make a wise choice in a mate without involving God in the process. In this, he does lead us to the right person for us. We might look at the divorce rate in our country and reject the idea of a soul mate. After all, if two people thought they were soul mates and now they can no longer stand the sight of one another, what does that say?

Far too many people go against their own conscience when marrying, having been swept away by an illusion of commitment with no real depth in the relationship. Their emotions paint an unrealistic picture of how wonderful their marriage is going to be—an effortless daily honeymoon. As soon as reality sets in and the relationship becomes work, they decide their spouse wasn't their soul mate after all. So, they go in search of the person they believe they were really meant to be with.

In contrast, I believe my husband became my soul mate—and sole mate—the moment he slipped a ring on my youthful finger over thirty years ago. I committed to love him through the peaceful times and the struggles, no matter which came our way. I pledged to hang in there, even when the

> From a young age Michelle had strong godly character, and she was sweet but not flirty. I respected how she contributed to discussions about the Bible and how she challenged me to want to be my best. I knew Michelle was the right person for me because we balanced out each other's strengths and weaknesses. —*Phil*

infatuation wore off and I didn't feel as in love. We committed our souls to God, the One who is the ever-present glue that binds us together.

God did have the two of us set apart for one another, not by a divinely determined algorithm based on our wish lists for a spouse but according to God's knowledge. God knew I would need a patient man who knew how to handle me when I flipped out—do I have to admit that this happens? I would need a kind and gentle husband to soothe my rough edges and prickly personality traits. And Phil would need a wife who would pep talk him through days of raising support for full-time ministry and keep a well-organized home to balance his childlike, fun-loving spirit (which manifested itself often during the writing of this book). God brought us together in his wonderful timing.

The future husband I created in my mind when I was fourteen or fifteen years old was founded on foolish immaturity. God brought me a man who had a depth I couldn't have imagined at that young age. As we've matured together, we've grown and expanded the qualities we had only in small amounts at first. It took time for us to become the people we each wanted in the other.

A soul mate does not mean a perfect mate. It means our souls are both committed and dependent on God to help us get through every imperfection we bring to the union. It means we work through our conflicts and stay true to the promise we made.

We aren't like two kids in love anymore. We sit in our recliners at night, one sleeping, the other on her laptop writing blog posts and book chapters. We poke each other all night long to get the other to stop snoring—when we sleep in the same room (see chapter 10). We argue sometimes and act selfishly. Yet, we're more soul mates now than ever before because the grace of God has carried us through so much.

We didn't find our soul mates. We became them.

The Process of Growing Together

When the emotional infatuation wears off and suddenly, you're staring across the table at someone who slurps their cereal and smacks their pizza, the honeymoon is probably over, but the marriage isn't.

This is where too many couples make a mistake. They think that when the feeling of romance and butterflies in the stomach wear off, the marriage has gone sour. They discover that the very things that were cute and endearing five years ago are now annoying and obnoxious. For example, Phil is a fun-loving guy with a dry sense of humor. He would much rather provide comic relief than teach a class or lead a Bible study.

His take on life makes him fun to be around and an enjoyable person. He doesn't complain much, and he encourages the best in people. But sometimes—and especially after thirty years of it—his playfulness doesn't feel very much like adult behavior. His approach can remind me of a junior high boy, minus the stinky hair and gangly feet. Thank goodness! He will insert a humorous response to avoid difficult subjects or tough decisions. And suddenly I'm annoyed.

"Could you just be a grown-up for ten minutes? I'm tired of being the only adult in this house." (Note the dramatic exaggeration here, since he goes to work for forty to fifty hours each week and does adult things.)

"Could you learn to relax and have a little fun once in a while? Your forehead wrinkles kind of weird when you're mad." (Note that the comeback doesn't exactly help the situation.)

"Someone has to be responsible," I say. This is where my smartwatch might sound to alert me that my pulse has increased too much. Perhaps someday it will record this as a workout.

> Every relationship has its challenges. We know that there are giant challenges in some marriages, and we don't want to downplay that. We don't want to make this too simplistic and make it sound like there is a simple solution to every conflict. But we have also observed that sometimes marriages break up over disagreements they could work out. —*Phil*

Does life have to be all serious with no play? Maybe it can be both. Maybe his annoying humor is a zap of fun, like snapping your fingers to break the tension for a Doberman that is fixed to attack. Yes, that's me sometimes. Phil is the golden retriever that gallops in, tail wagging, ready to lick your face.

There is a balance between fun and seriousness that makes life better. If you've lost the ability to have fun together, maybe you have also forgotten how to act like soul mates.

Unleash the Fun

Typing "unleash the fun" above made my palms sweat. I am the fun police. The idea of unleashing fun sounds dangerous and like a recipe for trouble. Yet I know it's important because laughter keeps us close. But let's agree that fun needs to have boundaries. For example, there is an appropriate time to be serious. Phil is working on this—forever. But I would venture that marriages suffer more from a deficit of fun than they do from an abundance of it.

When was the last time you said to your spouse, "We have way too much fun in our life"? Even fun-loving people like Phil can lose their natural tendency toward fun when certain feelings take center stage in a relationship. If some of the following—or all of them—are present in your relationship it can hinder your sense of fun and damage your connection at the soul level. We share these because we have been there! Let's look at three characteristics we have experienced that you might have too: feeling apathetic, bored, comfortable.

Did you see what I did there? Apathetic. Bored. Comfortable. Let's get back to the basics and look at the ABCs.

A – Apathetic. Apathy is toxic to a marriage, and it doesn't happen overnight. It's a buildup of emotions that leads to one or both spouses checking out. It's like getting a divorce but staying in the same home. It's often our way of protecting our own emotions, and getting past apathy means being vulnerable to getting hurt. I remember feeling apathetic at some points in our relationship. It's when I didn't feel like trying because I wasn't sure there was anything to strive for anyway. Here are some ways to process apathy if you're in the middle of it:

> Dealing with serious things is my awkward zone. I try to avoid it. But keeping a marriage healthy takes some serious work, and even if it isn't always fun. Michelle came up with some creative ideas for overcoming apathy, boredom, and comfort. I'm all for adding fun to help break some of the tension of working through the more difficult moments. –*Phil*

- Practice giving out more compliments than complaints.

- Check your criticism and ask, "Is this comment necessary?" (Sheesh, there were some days when if I had removed my criticism, I would have been silent all day.)

- Make a list of everything you love about your spouse, or what you loved before. Then work at focusing on those qualities.

- Do more together than you do on your own. If all of your free time involves something that is with other people, it's time to get back to a balance. It might take some work to find common interests again, but get creative!

- Pray together. This isn't an easy step for everyone. Maybe you'll have to write out prayers in a journal and let the other read it, especially if your heart is too vulnerable to pray aloud together. You'll find something that works for you. Be careful not to compare your quantity of couple's prayer with that of other people you know. Comparison can bring us right back to apathy.

> Marriage is messy. But it's like when I look under the hood of a vintage Jeep. It's a mess of wires and hoses and motor oil and road dust, but when it runs, it's beautiful. –*Phil*

- Pursue each other and each other's interests. At first it might feel one-sided, but keep pursuing as long as you have your marriage. This means setting aside your personal pain and rejection to sacrifice pride for the sake of your marriage.

- Renew your vows with a small family gathering—or a big one if you can afford it!

B – Bored. If either of you is bored in your relationship, these ideas might spark some fun:

- Make a list of fun, no-cost things you can do together. Keep the list handy for when you can't decide what to do for a date night.

- Get out a kids' game such as Candyland or Chutes and Ladders. Play it together and change the rules as you wish.

> I consider it my job in our marriage to make sure our relationship is never boring. Michelle can count on me for daily goofiness, flirty text messages, and random comments. –*Phil*

- Leave notes on a whiteboard or chalkboard for each other.

- Text each other randomly during the day. These are not the reminder texts such as, "Pick up

Junior at 4:00." These are fun and thoughtful, a link to an article, a funny cartoon, a sweet note, etc.

- Make non-sexual physical contact throughout the day—with no expectations.

- Take a day trip somewhere with just the two of you. Take turns planning your day trips and incorporate something you know your spouse will love.

- Surprise each other with whatever floats your boat—buy a gift, cook a favorite meal, hop into bed naked and watch your husband's jaw drop, buy her flowers, clean up the kitchen. Get creative!

C – Comfortable. Often, we get into a comfortable rut. Is this familiar? Get up, go to work, mow the lawn, eat supper, watch a show, watch the news, go to bed. If you have children, their routines factor into the mix. We go through the motions without thinking. Sometimes, we get so stuck in the rut that we don't notice when our spouse is having a rough time. We think everything is okay, until surprise—he or she moves out without warning. That's an extreme example but one that many couples know as their reality. Here are some ways to avoid getting too comfortable:

- Change up your routine or add in a date night.

- Do one of each other's regular chores without expecting thanks.

- Express gratitude to each other for little things that are part of your normal routine. Make a practice of noticing what your spouse does without being asked.

> I'm way more spontaneous than Michelle is. I think it sort of freaks her out when something isn't on her calendar. —*Phil*

- Leave the lights on to make love, even if you're self-conscious.

- Tell each other what you admire about the other.

- Be spontaneous, even if you hate surprises.

Fun is a choice. If you tell yourself something isn't fun, it won't be. Love is a choice. If you tell yourself you're not in love, you won't be. I have one other ABC to share about being sole mates and soul mates: Always Be Considerate.

We have the best role model ever, seen in the attitude of Jesus. He gave up his own comfort to serve others and lived sacrificially:

> Is there any encouragement from belonging to Christ? Any comfort from his love? Any fellowship together in the Spirit? Are your hearts tender and compassionate? Then make me truly happy by agreeing wholeheartedly with each other, loving one another, and working together with one mind and purpose.
>
> Don't be selfish; don't try to impress others. Be humble, thinking of others as better than yourselves. Don't look out only for your own interests, but take an interest in others, too. You must have the same attitude that Christ Jesus had. (Philippians 2:1–5)

I love to watch Hallmark movies; they're my Saturday go-to when I want to unwind while I fold laundry. But I've realized they aren't a great source for navigating through real-life relationships. And they're predictable enough that I can narrow the hundreds of movies down to a handful of plots:

- Girl comes back to visit relatives and runs into hometown guy from high school who is SO much better than the snobby rich lawyer she's engaged to. Lawyer shows up right when she's getting cozy with hometown boy, and girl has to make up her mind.

- Widower with a daughter meets girl who is a writer or radio personality. Daughter instantly bonds with girlfriend and never gets sassy or acts like a real child.

- Widow with a son meets soldier and is surprised she's falling for another solider. Soldier wins her heart when he teaches her son how to play baseball. Golden retriever plays a role in sealing the deal. Bonus plot: soldier might also be secret royalty.

- Guy and girl are bitter enemies in a bakeoff or decorating contest but then find true love and cooperate with each other to win the championship. Best friend takes care of all of the real-life details, apparently for very little pay.

Life isn't that predictable. Phil is not the secret king of a small country. He didn't sweep me off my feet and rescue me from a city life and plant me in a perfect bed-and-breakfast setting to fulfill my lifelong dream of becoming a party planner or the owner of a flower shop.

> Who is she kidding? There is one plot. They always live happily ever after. And they drive Jeeps in a lot of the movies. That's pretty cool. How do they get so much time off work? *—Phil*

Our story of becoming sole mates is more like this: Boy sees girl at church. Girl snubs boy for a few months. Boy scrapes together a few coins for a first date, then they get married and live in a trailer home in a neighborhood dubbed "Parkview Penitentiary." Boy and girl eventually upgrade to a 1000-square-foot home and have two children and mingle happy memories with arguments after the children go to bed at night. They move a few more times and upgrade to a 100-year-old home, launch their children into the world, and celebrate some milestone anniversaries. Boy and girl gradually learn how to become more like Jesus and wish they could undo a few years, but live gratefully ever after for sticking it out together.

I'm pretty sure your story isn't a Hallmark movie either. I pray that as God works in each of you and you become more like Jesus, that you'll discover unexpected surprises that sweep away apathy, boredom, and comfort. I pray you'll have sweet moments that show why God has brought you together. As you practice being sole mates, he will show you how to be soul mates.

Tune-Up Time

- Describe which of these you struggle with the most: apathy, boredom, comfort.
- Discuss how you would define "soul mates."
- Make a list of ten to twenty date ideas that you could realistically do (that fit with your time and budget).
    * Write these on slips of paper and put them in a jar that you can draw from when you need an idea.
    * For fun, decide that you will do whichever one you draw.
- Fill in the blank. When I get angry, I tend to _____.
- Describe an alternate way to react when you're angry that could improve the health of your marriage.
- Agree or disagree: I'll do anything to avoid potential conflicts with my spouse. Discuss how you think your reaction affects your relationship for good or bad.
- Agree or disagree: I sometimes feel apathetic about our relationship, and I don't feel like trying to fix it. Discuss your responses.
- Agree or disagree: I am bored in our relationship. Discuss a strategy to move past boredom.
- Agree or disagree: Our relationship is in a comfort zone, and I long for some variety. Discuss what this means for you as a couple.

- Agree or disagree: I love spending time together.

  * My favorite thing to do with my spouse is_____.
  * If we could do one new thing together, it would be_____.

- Which one of you is the most spontaneous in your relationship? Make a plan for how you can swap roles within the next week:

  * For the one who is more spontaneous, plan out a date your spouse would appreciate and schedule it waaaay ahead (which, for you, probably means two days ahead).
  * For the one who is scheduled and buttoned up, surprise your spouse by agreeing to an unplanned activity. Drop everything and just have fun.

Chapter Twelve

LAUGHTER, THE LANGUAGE OF HARMONY

One of the ways we have learned to survive tense moments in our household is by the application of humor. It isn't always well timed or welcomed, but often, it's just what we need. It helps me to shift my thinking, jar my brain, and stop the momentum on negative thoughts—thoughts that often lead to nagging, yelling, criticism, or some other dysfunctional action.

Phil sometimes tries to be funny too often and isn't serious when we need to have an uncomfortable discussion. But for the most part, he has taught me how to have fun. I tend to take life too seriously. With practice, I have learned to look for glimmers of joy and fun in everyday disappointments.

For instance, I like to have a clean house. I grew up with clean standards—my mother was a pro at keeping a spotless home—but real life doesn't always provide the time to clean, and I don't have the energy to keep up with it all even

> There is no such thing as too much fun.
> —*Phil*

when I do have the time. Instead of cleaning here and there, I'm pretty likely to get to a point where I can't stand it any longer, and then, rather than putting my energy toward cleaning, I'll have a meltdown that involves a tirade about how I live with the messiest people on earth and no one knows how to clean up after themselves.

But when I shift my mind into humor gear—you have that gear too; it's right after neutral but before meltdown—then I can laugh and skip right past the meltdown. In humor gear, I can leave love notes to my husband on the coffee table, written in dust. I can trace a message on the grimy television screen, "Please record The Voice." I'm able to see the clumps on the hardwood floor under the piano and say, "Oh, the bunnies are multiplying like rabbits around here." Dust bunnies have even more babies than the bunnies in my back yard (which are pretty impressive in their multiplication, I might add).

> She doesn't appreciate my love notes written in spilled sugar on the kitchen counter. *–Phil*

In case you were thinking of rescuing me, please, don't send Merry Maids over until I can transfer my to-do list from the dust on my desk to my smartphone; I need those items!

I was at a conference, and around the lunch table women were discussing how often we should vacuum. Women do that. They talk about cleaning. For the husbands reading, this probably sounds ridiculous when there are topics such as football scores, exhaust manifolds, how often you should change the oil in your car, and other more interesting things to hash out, right?

Women set up standards and then dare to compare with each other, as if my method is the world's best one, and everyone else should do it the same way. We have a way of shaming each other with elusive statements, sometimes.

"Who has time to clean?" I lamented.

One woman at the table said, "It's better for allergies if you vacuum often."

"Claritin works for me," I said. Sarcasm. Smart aleck. It's where I go when I feel weak.

Blank stares from all around.

Maybe I should have mentioned a meme I once saw that said, "Dust: it's what gives a home a warm and fuzzy feeling." Sometimes I know when to keep my mouth shut.

There are other sayings that show up on social media memes. I'm saving them for the right lunch conversation:

- Another one fights the dust.
- Instead of cleaning the house, I just turn down the lights.
- Behind every good marriage is a good house-cleaning service.
- You know that amazing feeling you get when you go to bed knowing your house is clean? Yeah. Neither do I.

> Has any woman ever started an argument with a husband who was cleaning a toilet, vacuuming, dusting, or emptying the dishwasher? I think I might be on to something, here. –*Phil*

Laughing calms me. It brings down my pulse and blood pressure. It changes my perspective and somehow what was so frustrating is now no big deal.

Know What Is Funny

Before we go too far—and you know that humor can always go too far—let's be sure to establish what is funny and what is not. I'm not trying to insult your intelligence. But sometimes what we think is funny is not. We use a lot of sarcasm at our house. Some families have rules against sarcasm, since it can sometimes be outright disrespectful and hurtful. To use sarcasm well, it's important to have a strong sense of what is funny, what is not, what is appropriate, and what should be saved for our private thoughts.

Even the Bible has guidelines about timing laughter appropriately, so it's important to know not to go all willy-nilly with jokes without thinking about our spouse's feelings. "A cheerful heart is good medicine, but a broken spirit saps a person's strength" (Proverbs 17:22). Poorly timed humor can break someone's spirit.

I have observed other couples and mentally noted the contrasts in humor. Here is a good tip: if both of you are not laughing, it wasn't funny or appropriate. If your husband's face is stoic and serious when you tried to break the tension with sarcasm, you might owe him an apology. If your wife looks as if she could burst into tears in two seconds, say you're sorry and offer a hug. She didn't think your comment was funny. These are not okay:

- **Insulting your spouse in front of guests.** Jokes about her cooking or his growing mid-section are awkward. Observe the difference between how your guests laugh. If it produced a belly laugh from *both* husbands and wives in the room, it's probably genuine laughter. But if only one gender laughs, or if the others give an awkward half-chuckle followed by uncomfortable looks at each other, you were out of line.

- **Using humor to point out sensitive subjects.** Her post-baby belly, gray hair, wrinkles, or lumpy thighs are off limits. For. Ever. His ongoing job search, weight, his inability to fix the toilet, or his mother might be sensitive topics. Phil had a difficult time in school; some of his teachers were harsh, and the kids teased. Anything related to academic intellect is a no-zone area for jokes in our relationship. For me it is weight. I have always been a little on the husky side. I wouldn't say huge. More like solid in a farm-girl, sturdy sort of a way. (I should have probably considered shot put in track and field sports in high school.) I have always compared myself to other girls, and I remember how boys teased me in school for being curvy. That is a no-way-dude zone for jokes from my husband. I'm so self-conscious of my weight that it would crush me to have him make fun of it.

- **Teasing with any motive but fun.** We have to check our own motives before using humor. If my motive is to put down my husband or to make myself look superior, then it isn't good-natured teasing. If our intent is to be a mean girl or a bully, it isn't appropriate.

- **Approaching a serious topic with a joke.** Here is a hypothetical example. If we need to have a conversation about how much I'm gone for commitments to other people—friends, coffee dates, retreats, appointments—and Phil doesn't want to bring it up for fear I'll be defensive, he might attempt to make a joke about it: "Do I know you? I hardly see you around here anymore. What is on your social agenda today? Tea with the queen? Volunteering for a charity to cure cancer? World peace?"

  However, this usually results in a defensive response, since I can see right through his attempts. Which leads him to decide that if I couldn't handle the topic as a joke, I'd have a meltdown to beat all meltdowns if he brought it up for reals.

  Which isn't true. Because if he explained it this way, I might receive it better: "Michelle, I've noticed you have a lot going on and you've said you wished you had more down time. I wish we could have a little more time to have quality conversation together, too. What would it take to make that happen?" You see, there he is speaking my love language—quality time—and he's looking for solutions, rather than criticizing.

- **Laughing *at* your mate instead of *with* them.** If I spill my iced coffee all over the front of my outfit and I'm laughing about it, that's fine. But if I just ruined my favorite outfit by spilling a bottle of nail polish all over it and I'm about to cry, I want empathy. If he spends a whole day working on the engine of his truck and ends up with a leftover part that will require several additional hours of ripping things apart again to put back, Phil wants a bowl of Peanut Butter M&Ms and a cup of coffee, not my laughter.

- **Accusing your spouse of being too sensitive.** If he or she is hurt, this is their reality. Maybe they are extra sensitive, but that doesn't make it right to play into that and use it as an excuse for being hurtful.

> It's never helpful to act as if something is wrong with the other person if our humor wasn't received well. It's a good indication that we might need to pause and apologize. Like for example, when we were newlyweds and at a family Thanksgiving dinner for her side of the family, and someone asked me about Michelle's cooking. I turned to her and said, "Hon, what's that thing you make with the raisins and the flakes with milk on top?" Yeah. I apologized. *—Phil*

Learn Each Other's Laugh Language

In the same way each of us has a love language—a particular thing that makes us feel loved—I think each of us has a laugh language too. Study each other and learn what makes you laugh. Phil comes from a family that tells corny jokes. I've mentioned this often in the book, so you know I'm not kidding! He tells the same ones over and over again. He laughs at them every stinking time.

I cringe and groan when he starts one, but corny jokes are part of his laugh language. He's especially delighted when someone who has never heard the joke before has a knee-slapping reaction. It's a bonus if it makes them laugh until they cry.

I like clever combinations of words and puns. We both like funny videos. We also both like humorous stories. Phil has enough material from his growing up years that he could do his own stand-up show—if he liked crowds or microphones. I found high school to be fairly mundane and somewhat boring. Essentially, I was there to get good grades and win awards. But Phil had a different approach: to make people laugh.

This also meant more than the average amount of trips to the principal's office, getting kicked out of class, and other memorable moments. He says it's a good thing we didn't attend the same high school. He's probably right. I wasn't too impressed by guys like him in class. I called them names in my head. (I confess this now and ask for absolution.) Phil wasn't drawn to my type either. Boring! And yet here we are, proving that opposites really can make a great marriage.

Sometimes during our small group Bible study, Phil will tell a story that I've never heard. After knowing him for more than thirty-five years, he is still coming up with new stories that make me laugh.

Your sense of humor doesn't need to be the same as each other's. An article in *Psychology Today* says, "For long-term relationships, such as in marriages, couples generally share a similar sense of humor—although similarities in sense of humor are not associated with greater marital satisfaction, nor with longer marriages."[5]

> Here's an example of my kind of humor. On Black Friday, my son Austin and I were hauling–you guessed it–a Jeep on a trailer when we blew a tire on trailer. We were near a Walmart that had a tire center, so we prayed we would be able to get a new tire right away. The man working at the counter in the tire department looked less than thrilled about our arrival time. He looked at his watch, and said, "Gettin' here kind of late, aren't you boys?"
>
> I resisted the urge to say, "Yeah, me and the boy were home watching football at 7:00 p.m. on the busiest shopping day of the year, and I said, 'Hey, how 'bout you and me run down to Walmart with that blown-out tire we have out in the shed and get it fixed before they close at 8:00?'"
>
> I saved my sarcasm for a private laugh with Austin. *–Phil*

It's also important to note that men and women respond to humor differently. Phil's use of humor as a way of avoiding conflict is in line with the way other men operate, according to the study mentioned above. "Two studies show the disparate function of humor for men and women. For men, humor might serve as a way to distract from dealing with problems in the relationship, perhaps in an attempt to reduce their own anxiety. Women, on the other hand, may use humor to create a more relaxed atmosphere that can facilitate reconciliation."

I believe the key is learning what you both like and making an effort to speak that language while timing it appropriately. It takes practice, but based on our experience, you'll have instant gratification when your spouse responds with laughter.

There are numerous ways of categorizing the types of laugh languages we speak, but a study from a well-known relationship website gave six types that provide a helpful summary:[6]

- **Physical Humor:** Physical acts such as scaring others, pranks, or falling. Think of slapstick comedy. Men tend to find this funnier than women—does that surprise you? This came in as the number one type of humor in the study. I could have figured that out from one episode of *Funniest Home Videos*.

- **Bodily Humor:** This includes toilet humor and bodily functions, as well as humor that is sexual in nature. Surprisingly, this isn't only funny for junior high boys. I sympathize if your spouse thinks you will be impressed with burping the alphabet.

> Just for the record, I don't do potty humor or fart jokes. But no criticism if that's your thing. —*Phil*

- **Self-Deprecating Humor:** Where an individual makes fun of themselves and their shortcomings to make others laugh. Many stand-up comedians use this. Women found self-deprecating humor funnier than men did in the study.

- **Wordplay Humor:** This includes puns and emphasis on unexpected meanings and usage of certain words. More women appreciated this style than men. Now we're speaking my language!

- **Surreal Humor:** This is based on obviously illogical and exaggerated stories. Again, many stand-up comedians use this style in making observations about real life and then exaggerating them. Women enjoyed this type of humor more than men. Guys, don't say a word about women and exaggerating or drama here. Just move along.

- **Dark Humor:** Making light of people and subjects that are considered serious or taboo. The movie *Weekend at Bernie's* comes to mind here (the entire plot centers around two men who use their boss's corpse like a puppet to convince people he is still alive). Men were found to be the bigger fans of dark humor.

Guys, I speak for women here; we know how to laugh at ourselves, and we aren't as impressed by your fart jokes as you want us to be. Gross and vulgar isn't usually our style. But we can still appreciate how it entertains you. We will try our best to find it funny when you show us a video of your massive wipeout on your dirt bike. In return, we love it if you will laugh when we pull our ponytail across our upper lip and say, "I mustache you a question."

According to the study, levels of education did play a role in sense of humor. More educated people weren't as impressed by physical humor and surreal humor, but they were impressed by wordplay humor. And kids make us more open to self-deprecating humor, probably because when you're standing there with baby food in your hair and poop stains on your shirt, there isn't much else left to do but laugh at the picture. And, no doubt, sleep deprivation makes everything seem funnier than it is.

> My laugh language might be described as dry, which I think means people who aren't really paying attention might miss the moment. I say a lot of things under my breath, and I'm more creative than I might get credit for. I consider an eye-roll a big compliment. I do like sarcasm and exaggeration. *–Phil*

Closing Tips

Become good students of each other. Watch your spouse with his or her friends and observe what makes them laugh. Pay attention to which parts of a movie, or which types of movies make them laugh. Give each other the courtesy of laughing when something is funny. Rolling the eyes or ignoring isn't great for your marriage. Neither is a blunt commentary. "That's dumb" has never served either of us well in our marriage.

> If I find a funny pun on social media and share it with Michelle, it shows that I understand her sense of humor and care enough to at least attempt to speak her language. Or if she finds a video with exaggeration or a motorcycle wipe-out, it speaks my language when she shares it with me, and it tells me she thought of me. –*Phil*

If you've ever watched a comedian struggle with a tough-sell crowd, you know that eventually they give up trying. Part of being funny is getting a response from the crowd. So, give each other the gift of a response. Be the "crowd" of one and appreciate one another's attempts at humor. Even great comedians need practice.

Sometimes, the natural look on our face when we're thinking about nothing at all tends toward grumpy. I don't love it when Phil takes a picture of me when I'm not looking and he texts it to me. Often, I don't look the least bit friendly! It takes practice to make it pleasant, so work on having a smile on your face more often. It will lead to a lot more fun in your relationship.

> My way of describing the look on her face when Michelle is watching TV or chilling out is that she sometimes looks like Grumpy Cat. Did I say that out loud? –*Phil*

Create humor together. Don't work too hard at being a comedian, but instead work at laughing together. Making a joke out of everything or trying too hard to be silly is too much. Obvi.

After time, you'll spend more years together than you were apart. Phil and I have been together for more than thirty-five years and I was twenty when we got married. There are more stories and memories we have in common now than before. We have created funny memories together, and the retelling of them brings us continued laughter.

Over the years, I've learned that the Golden Rule of doing unto others as you'd have them do to you is not just a proverb, and it isn't a suggestion; it's God's requirement. The biggest transition has been learning how to think less about whether or not Phil was put on earth to make me happy, but in seeking what will bless him. Since corny jokes bless him, I'll continue working on that language. Here's one for you babe.

Why did the motorcycle tip over?

It was two tired.

Why was the chef arrested?

He was caught whipping cream and beating eggs.

—Phil

Tune-Up Time

- Which type of humor do you think is your spouse's top language: physical, bodily, self-deprecating, wordplay, surreal, or dark?
- Describe something that makes your spouse laugh.
- What movie do you find funny, and you could watch it over and over again?
- Share a funny experience that you have never shared with your spouse before. (Maybe skip it if it's about an ex.)
- Describe a time when you were hurt by something your spouse thought was funny. Allow for open sharing without defending or giving a rebuttal. If your spouse was hurt, the pain was real.
- Try to remember a time when you both laughed so hard together you lost your composure. Describe as many details as you can remember. What made it funny?
- Describe a typical scenario in your relationship where one of you might use humor inappropriately to cope. Discuss a better way to respond that would lead to progress and growth.
- Describe a typical scenario in your relationship where humor could be helpful. Talk about ways that humor could ease tension and help you relax in the midst of conflict.

Faith

Chapter Thirteen

SPRINTS AND SPIRITUAL HURDLES

I met Phil at church when I was fifteen years old. If you're going to meet a potential spouse anywhere, church is a great place for that— not that it's some sort of dating club or anything. But if someone is going to look for a person of faith, that's a good place to start. A guy with a solid Christian faith was the number one item on my list for potential husband material. So, meeting at church gave me an immediate opportunity to observe that quality, even in its early and undeveloped stage.

In everyday life, teenage boys might be nice guys, act like gentlemen and all that, but it can be difficult to tell the depth of their faith. In between the typical teenage boy stuff, I could see a diamond-in-the-rough quality of spiritual stability, and I liked it. We didn't start dating until shortly after my sixteenth birthday. That's where we picked up in chapter 1. He noticed me long before I noticed him, so it wasn't as if I was watching him from afar and waiting for an opportunity. But when he did ask me out, my immediate thought was, "Huh, he's a really nice guy and he has qualities that other guys his age don't have."

As we started dating, I could immediately see something different about him. He was respectful of my parents' strict dating rules. We could see each other on a date twice a month and only on a double date with another couple. I had to be home by 11:00 p.m. If our plans changed, I needed to find a pay phone and let them know. Yes, a pay phone. Because back in the day, people didn't carry access to their parents around in their pockets.

> I'm glad Michelle could appreciate my charm as a teenager. Knowing she would be at youth group motivated me to be there. *–Phil*

Phil didn't try to hold my hand on the first date or make out in the back seat of his friend's car—our double date couple were the chauffeurs that night. He treated me like a person instead of an object. For an eighteen-year-old boy, that was impressive. He held doors for me—something he still does after thirty-five years.

Phil loved Jesus already then. His expression of his faith was often typical for his age, including sometimes goofing around at youth group or asking a smart-aleck question in Sunday School. But he also showed respect for authority and to his parents. I wasn't much more mature, but for a sixteen-year-old I did have a good Christian foundation. I had attended a Christian grade school and had started making my faith my own by studying the Bible and participating in a Bible study at my public high school. I wanted to get beyond superficial childhood picture book Bible stories and have meaningful conversations about faith and the doctrinal questions I wrestled with.

> Not to get Phil-o-sophical here, but questioning what some churches teach has pushed me to God's Word to study it more in order to really know what it says. *–Phil*

That started a journey of growing up together in faith. We were spiritual infants then, and our conversations now are much deeper than ever before. Phil reads more books and listens to more sermons and podcasts now. I have grown from knowing about God and taking a legalistic approach to the Bible into a discovery of how much

God needed to change in me. He's been softening and shaping my heart and mind as I learn to love people and let go of legalism. We have both grown in our love for God and our love for each other. But we have not always grown at the same pace.

Uneven Strides

There will be some phases in your marriage where one of you is at a different place spiritually than the other. If you started out with one of you a Christian and the other not, you have an even bigger gap. At first, it might have seemed as if that was no big deal to you. But as you have grown in your faith, you may have realized that the gap has widened. It isn't easy to be the one who goes to church alone every week.

Some of you started off at the very same place—non-churchgoers. But along the way, something changed, and one of you made a decision to follow Jesus. And suddenly there was a gap. Some spouses are content to let their husband or wife do their own thing, and it causes no conflict whatsoever. But even if it starts out that way, it often changes when children come along and you have to decide if they will go to church or not. And when they become pre-teens, they might argue, "If dad doesn't have to go to church, I'm not going either."

Perhaps you came from different denominational backgrounds. Again, this isn't always a challenge, but even in similar backgrounds there are potential conflicts. Consider this scenario: One spouse is from a Christian upbringing where they dedicate babies in a special ceremony and then people get baptized when they choose to do it them-selves as teens or adults. The other spouse is from an-other Christian background where they baptize babies and then they go through confirmation later. Both are Christians. But which will

> I made a decision to follow Christ at the young age of seven or eight. What really helped me grow in my faith as I grew up was attending Bible camp every summer. I have the opportunity now to be on staff at the same camp where I attended as a kid. As a teen, the youth conventions I attended with my youth group were also a big part of my spiritual growth journey. –Phil

you choose for your children? Will you reach a compromise together, or will extended family have a say? There are differences in the beliefs about the meaning of baptism between denominations as well.

All of these are important to consider before the marriage, but they are often the topics that we assume won't matter to us, and we discover well into the marriage that they do matter. That's when we begin the hard work of processing through the differences. This isn't a book about pre-marriage. It's about what to do if post-marriage some things come up that we didn't expect. There could be oodles of these in any marriage.

> I've been inspired by watching Michelle grow spiritually, but my best spiritual progress has come not when she has pushed me but when God led me in the direction that he wanted me to go. –*Phil*

Perhaps you began marriage with similar beliefs, and maybe you even grew up in the same church, but now your spouse has decided to leave the church. In a world of increasing struggle for genuine Jesus-like love and faith, there are people who have chosen to walk away from Christianity. My heart breaks for you. I acknowledge the painful path that you're unexpectedly walking if this has affected your marriage.

The Finish Line

When we think about spiritual growth and marriage, the most important factor that Phil and I have discovered is staying focused on the long-term goal God has called each of us to pursue, rather than on momentary pacing challenges between us. The Bible uses a metaphor for the Christian life by referring to it as a race in numerous passages. It's important to note it isn't a contest between us as individuals. Let's make it clear that we don't need to be hyper concerned about creating a competition between husband and wife for who is the best Christian.

Your pace along the way will vary. You might be in the spiritual marathon long before your spouse joins. Yes, that is more of a challenge in your relationship, but it doesn't stop you from moving forward. Let me give you an illustration that provides an image of how two people might have a different pace.

One summer, I decided I was going to brisk-walk a 5K for charity every month for eight months (avoiding winter months for obvious reasons). For one of those races, a friend agreed to join me.

Kim and I started the race together. I walked the whole thing at one pace—as fast as I could. Like shin-splint stride, with arms pumping and 80s rock songs blasting in my headphones. I know my speed varied throughout the race, but my pace was as fast as my legs would allow. Kim and I had agreed we would put in our headphones and each go at our own speed and then meet up again after the finish line. Kim is much braver than I am with pushing herself athletically. We have a similar build and similar height, but she set a goal to run parts of the race and walk parts of the race. You go girl!

Sometimes when you jog part of a race and then walk to catch your breath, your walking pace is a little slower than your normal walking pace. At least for me this is what happens. I jog, then suck air for a while and feel the throbbing in my calves and thighs. This makes me question how people ever run marathons, since 5K races are like the runner equivalent of the bunny hill for skiers.

Kim started off the race jogging, but after a bit she walked for a while. During that phase, I caught up to her and even passed her for a bit. Then she was ready to jog again, and she disappeared into the crowd of runners and walkers. This went on throughout the 5K. But the surprising thing was that when we approached the finish line, we were together again. We crossed the line with the exact same time as each other without trying to do that. Was either of our paces better? No. She enjoyed her run/walk and I enjoyed my walk. But the point is we were both focused on the finish and getting there at a pace that worked for us.

Your goal in life is spiritual maturity, which is fully achieved for each of us when we get to heaven. If you know someone who acts as if they have already arrived at full maturity, they took a shortcut on the marathon, and a race marshal is about to point out their flub. Spiritual maturity has to do with what goes on in our hearts, rather than on how well we can pretend to be holy. Jesus said, "Not everyone who calls out to me, 'Lord! Lord!' will enter the Kingdom of Heaven. Only those who actually do the will of my Father in heaven will enter" (Matthew 7:21).

Behind closed doors is where the real evidence of our spiritual maturity shows. I can fake out a lot of people at church, but there is no pretending when I'm home from church and I have my Sunday sweats or PJs on, and I turn off the filter on my tongue. We probably have a good idea of where each partner is in the spiritual race, but it's important that we be open to letting God take care of the changes in the other person while we focus on what he wants to do in us.

Let the pacing naturally flow while you cheer one another on rather than put one another down for where you are on the journey.

> Spiritual maturity is not about being able to talk about the Bible like a seminary professor. I would be headed for hell if that were required. Words like exegesis and hermeneutics are not part of my everyday chats with people. I'm a simple man. I like words such as gospel, love, grace, and peace. —*Phil*

The race begins with the gospel (the word gospel means "good news"). Have you made a step to commit your life to Christ?

> Let me now remind you, dear brothers and sisters, of the Good News I preached to you before. You welcomed it then, and you still stand firm in it. It is this Good News that saves you if you continue to believe the message I told you—unless, of course, you believed something that was never true in the first place.
>
> I passed on to you what was most important and what had also been passed on to me. Christ died for our sins, just as the Scriptures said. He was buried, and he was raised from the dead on the third day, just as the Scriptures said. He was seen by Peter and then by the Twelve. (1 Corinthians 15:1–5)

There are a lot of "gospels" out there, but not all are true. I want to make that clear, because if the wife bases her belief on New Age principles with a mix of religious thinking, and the husband bases his on the gospel of the Bible, you're running in different races and in different directions. Running in the wrong race can feel very spiritual and even look sort of Christian, but only those who do the will of God are in the race the apostle Paul talked about: "Don't you realize that in a race everyone runs, but only one person gets the prize? So run to win!...run with purpose in every step" (1 Corinthians 9:24, 26).

Once you establish your life based on the gospel of Jesus Christ, then the rest of life is the marathon that ends at heaven. And in that race, each step brings you closer and closer to the character and qualities of Jesus. The farther you go, the more like Jesus you become. But if you try to add in a mix of Christianity, New Age, Buddhism, and such into your life path, you veer off course and loop around on a detour that doesn't get you anywhere.

> Therefore, since we are surrounded by such a huge crowd of witnesses to the life of faith, let us strip off every weight that slows us down, especially the sin that so easily trips us up. And let us run with endurance the race God has set before us. We do this by keeping our eyes on Jesus, the champion who initiates and perfects our faith. (Hebrews 12:1–2)

The Race

If we could simplify the steps to moving forward toward spiritual maturity it would be this: pray, read the Bible, apply it to life, repeat. Prayer builds a relationship with God. It is a conversation with him and our connection directly to heaven. If you pray together as a couple, that is a wonderful way to share your pace. But not all couples are comfortable with this. The second step is reading the Bible. This can't move you forward without the third step; when we apply what we have studied, then we can grow beyond a collection of head knowledge. Someone can know a lot about God without having any spiritual maturity.

After we apply what we learn, we pray and ask God to show us more, to teach us more about who he is and who we should be. Of course, we pray more than that, but this is a simplified look at the process. We can actually complete this process every day, and even several times per day. Pray, read the Bible, apply it to life, repeat.

It is also important that we do this process in a community of other Christians—others who are in the same race. We cheer each other on, help each other understand what we read and how to apply it to life, and provide examples and inspiration for each other. This is a simplified description of what Christians call discipleship. Discipleship is how we teach others how to be followers of Christ so they can teach more people how to be followers of Christ, and so on.

As a couple, some parts of your Christian growth will take place in

> I have a couple of Christian friends that help me with accountability. It's easier to take advice from the guys sometimes than it is from my wife. They don't use as many "shoulds" when they talk to me. –*Phil*

your personal study of the Bible and in your personal prayer conversations with God. But it's also important to have growth that takes place together.

When Phil and I attend church together, we hear the same sermon taught from the Bible. On the way home, we often discuss our thoughts on the message and how it applies to us. This helps us to grow more than if we each did our own thing.

We also have different interests and styles of preaching and writing that we like. I love to read books. Phil reads books—but not too many. He prefers to listen to information, so he plays podcasts and sermons on his phone while he's working. I like to attend conferences and retreats with other women. Phil likes to take his Bible in a tree stand while hunting.

Each of these practices contributes to our growth in Christian faith. And every time we grow stronger in faith, the covenant bond we will talk about in chapter 16 becomes stronger. Why? Because God is a witness to our marriage—that's part of the covenant—and as a witness he can soften even the hardest of hearts.

> When we were first married, I was involved in church, but life and work distracted me some. I was also more swayed by the influence of some of my co-workers, which didn't pull me away, but it did make me complacent. I didn't study my Bible all that much, but I wasn't in a faith crisis either. In my early thirties, I experienced a growth spurt when I became more involved in church leadership. –*Phil*

Wait for Me!

I'm delighted when Phil goes through sprints in his faith. In fact, he's in one now as we're writing this book. He has all sorts of terms he wants to discuss related to theology that were never in his vocabulary before. As someone who would have a hundred college degrees if my budget had room for it, I enjoy discussions together about what he learns. I'm proud of him for his journey. But there are times when he's moving forward and I'm in one of my own personal challenges. It's like I've made a pit stop because I got a cramp in my side and watched him run on by. "Wait for me," I want to call out.

> My personality doesn't respond well to dragging or nagging. If a wife is reading this and you're desperate to see change in your husband, patiently do what helps *you* grow, but without forcing him. He will move forward when he is ready. If it helps, visualize how ridiculous it might look if you saw a woman at a 5K race dragging her 220-pound husband around by his arms or attempting to shove him from behind. The more she pushes, the more he digs in to stay put. —*Phil*

Eventually, I'll pick up my pace again and catch up. There have also been times when I'm in a spurt of spiritual growth and I long for him to be interested in what interests me. Ladies, we can't drag our husbands along in the race. Dragging, which rhymes with nagging, looks sort of like this:

- Acting like his conscience by saying, "You need to get right with the Lord."
- Leaving Bible verses on note cards all over the house, especially ones with judgy concepts.
- Putting Christian pamphlets on his nightstand.
- Playing sermons on the stereo when he's home to nudge him, when he isn't interested.
- Insisting on only listening to Christian music when you're in the car together.
- Bringing up church every week and begging him to go.
- Get the kids to ask him to go to church. "Please Daddy?"

1 Peter 3:1–2 says the wife whose husband is not on the same spiritual path as she is should accept his authority and respect him as a husband. She is to let her godly life speak without words as her husband observes

her "pure and reverent" life. This is how he is won over. Not with nagging and words, but with living out her faith as she applies what she learns in Scripture and continues to pray, read, and apply.

> Let us think of ways to motivate one another to acts of love and good works. (Hebrews 10:24)

> So encourage each other and build each other up, just as you are already doing. (1 Thessalonians 5:11)

We are to be each other's live-in cheer squad. I admit that far too often I'm not anywhere near as encouraging as I need to be for Phil. But I keep practicing and pushing myself to learn from my mistakes. And as I learn how to be more mature, God helps me to be a better cheerleader for my husband. Often, about the time I get a stride going, a hurdle comes along. I'm thankful I have a spouse who helps me get through those together, even if I trip over some hurdles and come out a little banged up. That's how we motivate each other to maturity. As God changes us, we become better encouragers for one another, and the pace picks up.

Imagine how it will feel when we reach the goal, heaven. We'll run through the finish line, arms raised in victory, sweaty and out of breath, but thankful for every moment—even the hard ones.

Husbands, it's our job to be the example in the home. This doesn't mean dictating or dominating, but instead encouraging our wife and kids on their spiritual 5K. I was a track runner in high school, and I remember what it was like to hear my dad encouraging me from the sidelines. I don't remember what he said, but I remember how I felt. His encouragement spurred me on–even when I was one of the slower runners. That's our role as husbands and fathers–to be encouraging, no matter the pace of our family members. –*Phil*

Tune-Up Time

- List all the ways you can think of where your spiritual journeys are similar. (Church denomination, theology, church attendance, etc.)
- List the differences in your spiritual journeys. (Baptism, church attendance, denomination, etc.)
- Use a stopwatch on your phone and give three minutes for each of you to describe a short summary of your journey of faith. Include how you came to know Christ.
- Take turns describing how you think God has changed your personal faith and spiritual maturity the most since you got married.
- Ask the question of each other: how can I support and encourage you in your spiritual race? Share two or three things.
- Tell your spouse what you are most inspired by in their spiritual growth process.

Chapter Fourteen

WE DIDN'T SEE *THAT* COMING

Phil and I have both had the occasion to watch our fathers care for our mothers in the middle of an "in sickness" phase of their relationships. For a year and a half, Phil's dad (Dan) took Joy to oncology appointments at the clinic and to special experimental treatments several hours from home, and he sat by her hospital bed in the living room, right up until the day she left us for heaven. He shattered any traditions they once had when he cooked meals, canned homemade jam so she didn't have to watch the raspberries rot on the vine outside her window, and he ushered hospice nurses and visitors in and out all day.

My mom (Ruth) spent some recovery time in a makeshift bed on the fold-out sofa in the family room while my dad (Jim) fumbled with sterile dressing changes as she talked him through it. She was a nurse, but now she was the patient. She lost her hair and lost her appetite. My dad kept up with milking the cows twice a day and doing field work while she recuperated from ovarian cancer and chemo.

In sickness and in health can create a faith crisis for some of us. When

Joy prayed for a miracle, it didn't come. That's tough to swallow. She left a legacy, but she wanted to live it in real life, not in the file cabinets of our memories or in photos.

Faith Crisis

Ours is one of those average, boring marriages that has not withstood one of these traumas yet. I say yet, because I have no idea what God has in store for our lifetime. While writing this book, we experienced one of the few "in sickness and in health" circumstances that we've ever had. I'll talk about that later in chapter 18.

My grandparents on my dad's side of the family buried a twenty-year-old son when he lost his life in a car accident. After his death, they learned that his girlfriend was expecting a baby. She moved on with her life, and eventually married, but my grandma never forgot her grandson who she got to meet but didn't get to see often. With her aching heart

> I remember when my mom first got her diagnosis. She was rightly sad and disappointed that there wasn't much hope for treatment. She was mad at God at first, but as she stayed connected to her anchor in God's Word and his promises, and she was an example of faith for her family and community. It was a hard lesson to help our boys understand too. *–Phil*

and longing to know more about the young boy as he grew, she had my grandpa bring her to school concerts when she saw mention of events in the newspaper, and she watched her grandson grow up mostly from afar.

I can't imagine the pain of losing a child at any age. It is a faith crisis when we can't answer the question: why?

Some marriages are so fragile that they can't survive this type of pain. Instead of pulling together, they push apart. Phil and I have examples in our families of strong people of faith who pulled together and drew closer to God even when the questions came.

But even with those examples, it is up to us to prepare for faith challenges. These are often outside of our control:

- Loss of a child
- Severe illness of husband or wife
- Dementia or memory loss
- Loss of a parent or sibling
- Military deployment
- Loss of income
- Lawsuit
- Bankruptcy
- House fire or business fire
- Car accident
- A child becomes a total care dependent because of disability
- A child is born with a genetic disorder
- A spouse goes to jail

We have talked in other chapters about some of the challenges that might come our way. But in this chapter, I want to focus on what shakes us up like nothing else and how to survive that sort of crisis as a couple. As I said, Phil and I haven't been through one yet, but these principles are proactive, for growing a marriage that is strong enough to withstand the attack.

Prepared for the Storm

Our foundation has to be in the right place. If it's in our own strength, then it will only go so far.

In the summer when Phil's mom got sick with cancer, they went on a camping trip with us to northern Minnesota to a state park that had a secluded private lake. The only dock on the lake was the one for the campground. It was as close to

> We shared my mom's diagnosis with our sons when we were at my parents' house, and we all gathered around to pray with our pastor. Our young boys knelt by the coffee table, and when they lifted their bowed heads after the prayer, the glass-topped table was dotted with their teardrops. Watching their grandparents walk a hard road was part of their own legacy of faith and an example they bring into their own marriages now. —*Phil*

looking like a wilderness lake as I was comfortable with.

One afternoon, Joy said she felt fine with us leaving her to rest with the kids at the campsite while Phil, his dad, and I went out fishing in the boat. The fishing wasn't that great, so Phil kept moving us around the lake to find the proverbial good spot. In my boredom, I decided to use some of our candy stash for bait, so I was fishing with a red Swedish Fish on my line.

As he'd been doing, Phil pulled the rope on the boat motor once again to move us to a new spot. But this time the motor coughed, sputtered, and billowed smoke.

"Yep. That's done." Phil has a way of not being clear sometimes.

"The fishing is done?"

"The motor is done. As in ruined."

I continued casting but hadn't snagged any fish.

Phil had a trolling motor on board, which has is an electric motor that runs off a marine battery. Trolling motors are made for a slow crawl around the lake for fishing, but not for speed. We started to head toward the dock, with the trolling motor moving us at the pace of a float in the Fourth of July parade.

Long before we reached the shore, the marine battery ran out of juice. Playing out like a terrible plot in a low-budget movie, there were storm clouds on the horizon and no other boats in sight.

Phil and his dad resorted to the only other means of getting us to shore—canoe paddles. Thankfully, Phil had recognized the importance of being prepared ahead of our adventure by at least having the man-powered oars in the boat. We didn't own cell phones or anything like that, so if we hadn't had those paddles, our only choice would have been to put down an anchor and wait for someone to come along. We made it back to shore.

> Sometimes you have to fish or cut bait. Just eat the Swedish Fish; don't fish with them. —*Phil*

No, Swedish Fish did not work for bait, either.

Even in good weather on a calm lake, a boat will drift. We have to have an anchor if we don't have a motor. Sometimes, the best you can do is to put down the anchor and wait for rescue.

Setting the Anchor

Think about how it feels to drift with no anchor on a small lake. Now imagine Lake Superior or the ocean. The writer of Hebrews warns against drifting away from the truth of God's Word:

> So we must listen very carefully to the truth we have heard, or we may drift away from it. (Hebrews 2:1)

If you're a Christian, then your anchor is in the hope of life after this one—the assurance of God's promise of heaven. Jesus is the rope that tethers us to that anchor. That tether is not a ball and chain; it is our freedom, our lifeline. As an anchor holds a boat in the right position during a raging storm—facing into the waves to prevent capsizing—likewise, having a secure anchor keeps our mind on God instead of life's waves. I like to think of Jesus as hope on a rope.

Hebrews tells us that Jesus is our forerunner, the one who carries our anchor into the harbor and secures it safely there. He's the one who can go ahead and make sure all is well and secure for us. This role is also given a different title in Hebrews. It says in multiple chapters there in Hebrews that Jesus is our High Priest. In the Old Testament, the high priest was the person who could go into the holy of holies to make the sacrifice for the people—the one who carried their offerings to God for them. He was the one that made the petition on their behalf, too.

I worked for nine years in the healthcare field, and I can tell you from observation that the people who had their anchor in a relationship with Jesus Christ had a peace in the middle of a storm that others didn't. They were the ones at peace before a major surgery or when given an unexpected diagnosis.

I saw death up close and served on the team that responded to assist with the code blue calls that came over the pager system within the medical complex. It made me think a lot about life and mortality. —*Phil*

Like that high priest, Jesus gives us a direct line to God. But we have to be tied to the anchor. If you've ever been out in a boat and gone to set the anchor only to watch the end that was supposed to be tied to the boat disappear beneath the water, you know how important it is to have it fastened in the right place. Ploop, and it's gone.

What does it mean to have your marriage anchored in the right place? Hebrews says it well:

> I have done that with an anchor. Only mine went kerplunk. *–Phil*

> This hope is a strong and trustworthy anchor for our souls. It leads us through the curtain into God's inner sanctuary. Jesus has already gone in there for us. He has become our eternal High Priest in the order of Melchizedek. (Hebrews 6:19–20)

Christ has anchored our hope of refuge in the very presence of God.

In addition to keeping a boat facing the right direction in a storm, an anchor also keeps it upright. It keeps the keel—the bottom part of the boat that looks like a backbone—from tipping over. Thus, where we get the expression "keeled over."[7] If your marriage keels over, you capsize. When you're anchored in God, you'll get tossed around a bit, but you won't capsize when life gets rough. Our anchor is not in these things:

- In our own ability or power
- In our behavior or being a good person
- In our confirmation, baptism, or symbols of faith
- In our achievements
- In our money or possessions
- In our relationships

Our hope and strength is in the Lord. If you look for it somewhere else, you'll keep looking for a place to drop anchor, and when you think you've found it, it will disappoint. And the next place you move to will be the same.

> Sometimes when I'm canoeing in the Minnesota Boundary Waters, I'll stop paddling to tie a hook on my line and I'll look up and the canoe has drifted toward rocks along the shore. It doesn't take much to drift.
>
> Being anchored to God isn't only for hard times; for me it's an everyday thing I do so that I'm prepared. I know trouble will come, since it's part of life.
>
> Being anchored means reading my Bible in the mornings and praying. It's knowing God's promises so they come to mind in difficult times. It really means making sure I don't drift away from God's truth. —*Phil*

You'll wander from place to place, job to job, person to person, church to church, always looking for something better, always looking for some harbor worthy of your anchor. But our anchor is in the hope of the cross.

The next time you see an anchor decoration over at Hobby Lobby—look for it—there is a cross in the anchor.

Hope from the Word

Scripture reminds us that we can weather the storm together with God. And it reminds us there can be hope and even joy in the middle of it. These are some of my favorite verses in the whole Bible:

> So be truly glad. There is wonderful joy ahead, even though you must endure many trials for a little while. These trials will show that your faith is genuine. It is being tested as fire tests and purifies gold—though your faith is far more precious than mere gold. So when your faith remains strong through many trials, it will bring you much praise and glory and honor on the day when Jesus Christ is revealed to the whole world.
>
> You love him even though you have never seen him. Though you do not see him now, you trust him; and you rejoice with a glorious, inexpressible joy. The reward for trusting him will be the salvation of your souls. (1 Peter 1:6–9)

Even though the fig trees have no blossoms,
and there are no grapes on the vines;
even though the olive crop fails,
and the fields lie empty and barren;
even though the flocks die in the fields,
and the cattle barns are empty,
yet I will rejoice in the Lord!
I will be joyful in the God of my salvation!
The Sovereign Lord is my strength!
He makes me as surefooted as a deer,
able to tread upon the heights. (Habakkuk 3:17–19)

Therefore, since we have been made right in God's sight by faith, we have peace with God because of what Jesus Christ our Lord has done for us. Because of our faith, Christ has brought us into this place of undeserved privilege where we now stand, and we confidently and joyfully look forward to sharing God's glory.

We can rejoice, too, when we run into problems and trials, for we know that they help us develop endurance. And endurance develops strength of character, and character strengthens our confident hope of salvation. And this hope will not lead to disappointment. For we know how dearly God loves us, because he has given us the Holy Spirit to fill our hearts with his love. (Romans 5:1–5)

As you work as a couple to anchor your faith, these are some qualities that will be important when a storm comes:

- **Unity.** When you have mutual faith in God, it puts you in a place for being one at heart.
- **Closeness.** Along with unity, there is a closeness that is hard to put into words. You're bound together inseparably.
- **Peace.** This is one of the biggest blessings I have noted for people who have faith in God. When life is full of questions, they have an unexplainable peace that God still has the answers. The Bible calls that the peace that passes all understanding (Philippians 4:7).

- **Joy.** I've watched people journey through cancer and more and still have a sense of joy in the Lord because they know happiness is an emotion, but joy is a choice.
- **Strength.** Faith gives us a sense of strength because we know we have God's power working in us and through us. This doesn't guarantee the outcome is always what we want, but we know God is bigger than us.

Your marriage will experience spiritual attack. Satan tried to disrupt the unity of the very first couple—Adam and Eve—by tricking Eve into causing Adam to stumble. If he has been at it that long, he will try to get your marriage to break apart. He's been successful with many couples. It is a battle between Satan and you, but you have God on your side when you are his children.

> I enjoyed listening to stories from couples who I met while working in healthcare. Their eyes lit up when I asked them to tell the story of how they met and how they got to fifty years of marriage. Their marriages inspired me as a young husband. I wanted to be the one telling the story someday of how I met Michelle. *–Phil*

Remember, you are not each other's enemy. When crisis comes, many couples turn against each other instead of turning toward each other for support. You will process stress in different ways from each other, so give each other room to do that, but please don't battle each other.

⁕

As I wrapped up some time away for writing this book, I was giddy with the joy of how much I had enjoyed my solitude and peace. The retreat center was in a forest of oaks, thus its name—Oak Forest Center, and I was able to stay during the off-peak season for retreats. The birds chirped all day long in the trees outside of my patio door. I wanted to stay forever. Some days, felt as if I had the place to myself. But on my last day, the maintenance guys started work outside of my window. They drove a skid steer up the hill with a cement mixer. I could see a project in the works. The voices of working men rose above the sound of the machinery as they set up their work equipment. The smell of diesel from the tractor exhaust drifted to my window. This was my cue to pack up and go home.

I decided it was the perfect reminder that if earth is too comfortable, we won't ever want to leave. And this world is not our home. Without pain and trials on earth, we would be content to make this the focus of our attention. But it is just uncomfortable enough to remind us that we have a home waiting for us after this life.

I'm thankful that God gave us each other for support while we're here. But every so often when life throws a challenge in your face, remind each other you aren't home yet. Be grateful together for the times when life feels like chirping birds and breezes in trees. But be thankful for the reminders in the seasons that feel like a tiny two-person sailboat in the middle of a squall on Lake Superior. That is part of life in our temporary home.

Losing my mom shook me. I still miss her after more than fourteen years. I don't want any reader to think we are minimizing their pain pretending to know how they feel. Instead, our message is more about how to prepare for the storms we know will come.

I've stood on the shores of Lake Superior after the gales of November have bashed the shoreline with crashing waves. These are the same kind of waves that sunk the Edmund Fitzgerald when I was a kid. (Michelle, can I play the song?)

I have seen whole chunks of sidewalk and small boulders moved by those waves. I'm glad I have hope in God. I believe he will hold me secure when a storm comes. –*Phil*

Tune-Up Time

- List some of the qualities about each other that you think makes you a great team.
- Discuss what you think would make you even better prepared to be a team that is ready to face a crisis together.
- Discuss what you think the most difficult part of a season of "in sickness and in health" would be (or already is) for you.
- What would you do together if you knew that one of you only had a year to live?
- What part about growing older together scares you?
- What part of growing older together makes you happy?
- Share briefly about another couple who modeled "in sickness and in health" well for you and how it inspires you.
- What is the best part about being together for the long haul?

Chapter Fifteen

I THOUGHT I FOUND TRUE LOVE

When I was a child, it was an extra special treat to get to watch *Hee Haw* in black and white and eat supper at TV trays in the family room. I remember a song that was played often on the show about true love and not being able to find it. As kids, we loved the line "Pfft! You was gone" that came at the end of the song because of the motions that went with it.[8] My brother and I would spray spit as we blew raspberries at each other by sticking out our tongues on the "Pfft!" part.

If I had to define true love without using a dictionary, I would say it has to be complete trust and willing sacrifice. It isn't a feeling. It's a knowing. True love doesn't disappear and pfft! you are gone.

It also isn't chemistry. It is possible to have great chemistry with someone you don't trust and for whom you wouldn't sacrifice anything. That's essentially an affair or a fling. There is a lot of emotion but no foundation. If you want to know a story of true love, there's one from the Bible that gives us an example.

> True love isn't really like it is in the movies. One of my favorite movies is *The Princess Bride*,[13] where a farmhand named Westley sets out to rescue his true love, Princess Buttercup, from obnoxious Prince Humperdinck. Death itself could not stop Westley's true love—well it wasn't death; according to Miracle Max, he was only "mostly dead," which is not the same as all dead. Spoiler alert: the farmhand gets the princess, which is the classic underdog wins situation. But real-life love isn't about rescuing or saving each other. It's about forgiving and sacrificing even when it hurts. Mostly forgiven is not the same as *all* forgiven. *—Phil*

Unconditional Forgiveness

Hosea and Gomer are a couple from the Old Testament in the Bible. I mentioned in chapter 8 that if Austin had been a girl, his name would have been Alyssa. Dallas would have been Erica. Surprisingly, we did not have Gomer on our list. Imagine parent-teacher conferences. "Gomer is having a hard time sitting still and using her inside voice." Or, "We really need to work on Gomer's punctuality in finishing assignments." Ironically, the name Gomer means "completion."[9]

> Technically, if we had a girl after our two sons, we *could* have named her Gomer, which means "completion." That would be a good name for the last child in a family. *—Phil*

Hosea was an Old Testament prophet whose name meant "Jehovah is salvation."[10] There's a book of the Bible named after Hosea, which he also wrote, that tells his story and contains the message God gave him for the people of Israel. A prophet was a lot like a preacher; the difference was God gave messages directly to him to give to the people.

A little back story about Hosea's job as a prophet: God viewed his chosen people of Israel in a figurative way as his wife (similar to how the new church is called the bride of Christ today). But his chosen people were pretty much like any other humans with their sinful way of living. They did whatever they wanted. They essentially committed adultery against God by worshiping idols, and this worship included all sorts of perversions. God saw this idol worship as equal to prostitution by his people. In Exodus 20:3 he said there were to be no other gods in his place, but the people had strayed from their relationship with God; basically, they were unfaithful.

During this time, God chose to speak through his prophet Hosea to warn his people. But he told Hosea to do an unusual thing.

> When the Lord first began speaking to Israel through Hosea, he said to him, "Go and marry a prostitute, so that some of her children will be conceived in prostitution. This will illustrate how Israel has acted like a prostitute by turning against the Lord and worshiping other gods."
> So Hosea married Gomer, the daughter of Diblaim, and she became pregnant and gave Hosea a son. (Hosea 1:2–3)

Hosea and Gomer had more children, and they all had unusual names that had meaning related to the prophecy for Israel—names God told Hosea to give them. Based on some of these names, the meanings of which are given in the book of Hosea, we might speculate as to whether or not these children were biologically Hosea's. Jezreel, Lo-ruhamah, and Lo-ammi had some interesting meanings to their names:

- A son named Jezreel – which means "God plants," after a fertile valley in north central Israel that had historical significance for the Israelites
- A daughter named Lo-ruhamah – which means "not loved"
- A son named Lo-ammi – which means "not my people," or "not my child"

This is sounding like an episode of the Jerry Springer show, right? "Let's bring out Hosea and his son, Not My Child." In Bible times, the names of children were a big deal. They were chosen because of the meaning.

Technically, we named our children "From the meadow dwelling" (Dallas) and "Great" (Austin). I guess that last one could be said with a little bit of sarcasm, as in, "Oh, greaaaat." But we meant it as, "Great!"

Hosea was obedient to God, even though God didn't gift him with an easy relationship with his wife. Have you noticed that sometimes when God gives you a task, he also gives you a challenge to go with it? God had a purpose in all of this for demonstrating his love.

> It does turn out that during a phase of colic, we did say, "Oh, greaaaat, he's awake again," a few times about our son whose name means "Great." *–Phil*

Despite their wayward wickedness, God loves his people Israel—then and now. And he wanted to show this to them through not only Hosea's words, but through his life. The book of Hosea doesn't fill in all of the details, but in chapter 2, God lays out the basic charges against Israel. And then in chapter 3, he tells Hosea to go and love his wife again even though she has committed adultery with another lover. "This will illustrate that the Lord still loves Israel, even though the people have turned to other gods and love to worship them" (Hosea 3:1).

So, he bought her back with silver, grain, and wine, and then he brought her home. Why did he have to pay to get her back? Remember she was a prostitute—and somewhere there was a pimp to whom she provided a paycheck. And what does this have to do with our marriages? Stay with me here. We're almost there.

Notice how beautifully God wove Hosea's story and his children's names into this message about Israel:

> [18] On that day I will make a covenant
> with all the wild animals and the birds of the sky
> and the animals that scurry along the ground
> so they will not harm you.
> I will remove all weapons of war from the land,
> all swords and bows,
> so you can live unafraid
> in peace and safety.

¹⁹ I will make you my wife forever,
  showing you righteousness and justice,
  unfailing love and compassion.
²⁰ I will be faithful to you and make you mine,
  and you will finally know me as the Lord.
²¹ "In that day, I will answer,"
  says the Lord.
"I will answer the sky as it pleads for clouds.
  And the sky will answer the earth with rain.
²² Then the earth will answer the thirsty cries
  of the grain, the grapevines, and the olive trees.
  And they in turn will answer,
  'Jezreel'—'God plants!'
²³ At that time I will plant a crop of Israelites
  and raise them for myself.
I will show love
  to those I called 'Not loved.'
  And to those I called 'Not my people,'
  I will say, 'Now you are my people.'
  And they will reply, 'You are our God!'" (Hosea 2:18–23)

Trust and Sacrifice

This story really isn't about the couple; it is about God and how he loves. But the point is that he has asked us to love like he does, so that makes it about marriage too. True love is sometimes painful. Remember how I said I would define true love as trust and sacrifice? Even when Hosea couldn't trust Gomer, he trusted God. He sacrificed his pride and his reputation for the sake of his marriage, and God restored it.

Trust and sacrifice come when we forgive. But how many times should we forgive each other? Shouldn't there be a limit, like a forgiveness bucket that eventually runs out? Not according to Jesus. In one of those moments that was similar to a child pumping a parent for boundaries on the rules, Peter asked Jesus how many times he was expected to forgive if someone wronged him. He wanted to know if seven times was enough.

I can imagine the thoughts in Peter's head. "There has to be a limit here. I mean, after I've forgiven someone seven times, surely, I deserve to

> I don't really like math, but I think Jesus was saying something like, "Stop keeping score of how many times you have forgiven." On another note: I haven't tested Michelle to see what would happen if I offended her more than seven times over the same issue. Or seventy times. —*Phil*

get revenge. Surely, I could have permission to punch the faces of James and John if those two keep doing the same stupid stuff over and over."

Nope.

Jesus said, not seven, but seventy times seven (Matthew 18:21–22). Jesus was simply saying, "to infinity and beyond." There is no end to forgiveness.

In a marriage, we have little opportunities to show true love every day. It isn't always what we say, but what we do. I can say "I love you," but if I follow it up with putting everyone else's needs in front of my relationship with my husband, my actions and words don't line up.

> Dear children, let's not merely say that we love each other; let us show the truth by our actions. Our actions will show that we belong to the truth, so we will be confident when we stand before God. Even if we feel guilty, God is greater than our feelings, and he knows everything. (1 John 3:18–20)

Forgiveness

We can show love in forgiving the little things—annoying habits or harsh words, criticism, thoughtless actions, rude attitudes, and broken promises. But some of them are bigger things—like what Hosea had to get past—a physical or emotional affair, unfaithful intentions, pornography, or broken trust.

Forgiveness means we absolve from guilt, even if the scars are still there or the wounds are still healing. Hosea and Gomer's story is about Israel, but it is also a picture of what God did for us through Jesus. We have all selfishly wandered from God and gone our own way, but God restored our relationship to himself by paying the ultimate price of the life of his Son, Jesus, to redeem us—just as Hosea paid a price for Gomer to redeem her.

There is something that motivated Phil and me over the years to practice forgiveness. It's the bond that was formed when we said "I do" because we made that promise in the presence of God. Because God ransomed us to save us from an empty life without hope or meaning, it motivates us to be different from the earthly norm. It motivates us to practice being holy—set apart and separated from sin[11]—as God's own children.

> I'm really glad "holy" doesn't mean perfect. It means I can keep practicing becoming more like God. —*Phil*

So prepare your minds for action and exercise self-control. Put all your hope in the gracious salvation that will come to you when Jesus Christ is revealed to the world. So you must live as God's obedient children. Don't slip back into your old ways of living to satisfy your own desires. You didn't know any better then. But now you must be holy in everything you do, just as God who chose you is holy. For the Scriptures say, "You must be holy because I am holy."

And remember that the heavenly Father to whom you pray has no favorites. He will judge or reward you according to what you do. So you must live in reverent fear of him during your time here as "temporary residents." For you know that God paid a ransom to save you from the empty life you inherited from your ancestors. And it was not paid with mere gold or silver, which lose their value. It was the precious blood of Christ, the sinless, spotless Lamb of God. (1 Peter 1:13–19)

Love Like Jesus Does

God didn't give his son as our ransom because we deserved it; God had mercy on us and didn't give us the punishment we deserved. And he showed grace by giving us a gift that we did not deserve, yet he gave it anyway. Our spouse might not deserve forgiveness or love, but we give it anyway because Jesus did. "We love each other because he loved us first" (1 John 4:19).

Dear friends, let us love one another, for love comes from God. Everyone who loves has been born of God and knows God. Whoever does not love does not know God, because God is love. This is how God showed his love among us: He sent his one and only Son into the world that we might live through him. This is love: not that we loved God, but that he loved us and sent his Son as an atoning sacrifice for our sins. Dear friends, since God so loved us, we also ought to love one another. No one has ever seen God; but if we love one another, God lives in us and his love is made complete in us. (1 John 4:7–12)

We used that last verse on our wedding invitations: "if we love one another, God lives in us and his love is made complete in us." We didn't know how difficult it would be to put the words of that Scripture into practice in real life. It's when we show true love to each other that God's love is brought to full expression in us. Because God is faithful, we can be faithful to each other. Because he forgives, we can learn to forgive. But it is a process. A looong one. We have learned to forgive the little things before they become big things. It's much harder to heal a gaping wound than it is a small scrape.

Building Trust and True Love

I don't know where you are in the process. Your journey might be really bumpy. If there has been an affair in your marriage, there is a process to rebuild trust and restore the relationship. If one spouse has lied, trust has eroded. We've observed friends who have salvaged marriages that we thought were goners! We've also seen some turn into a dumpster fire and end in a horrible way. As we have observed those that have survived the trauma, these are some of the common factors that have helped couples build trust and grow true love:

- **Commit to break off the affair.** This seems obvious, but you'd be surprised how many people think they can have both. This also is relevant for breaking off ties to pornography or the temptation or curiosity for it. Remove the temptation with accountability, an internet filter, or fasting from digital media altogether.

- **Devote yourselves to repentance, forgiving, and rebuilding.** A broken covenant (which we will discuss in the next chapter) can be restored if you choose to restore it. That isn't easy, but it can be done. It takes time.

- **Earn back trust.** Establish boundaries that will keep it from happening in the first place or from happening again. Keep your words and actions consistent to show you can be trusted. Even in our little conflicts, if Phil says, "I'll try harder," I push back. My trust is earned when I see action rather than empty promises. Earning trust takes consistent action built upon previous action.

  > I've watched friends go through painful affairs. Some of their marriages made it; some didn't. It's hard to imagine recovering from that, but yet it's possible since I've seen that happen when both partners were willing to work at it. —*Phil*

- **Be honest with each other.** Phil was honest with me when he and a friend were looking for bow hunting gear on the internet and a popup ad for naked women came up. He didn't know how to make the image go away. So, he shut down the computer and waited for me to come home. He explained what had happened. This was his first experience with targeted ads. (Internet bots know it is men who are usually shopping for bow hunting gear.) This also leads to the next tip.

- **Sacrifice.** Give up your own preferences for the sake of your spouse if it can build your relationship. When Phil was feeling exceptionally tempted by the stuff out there on the internet, he decided he didn't want to let his curiosity get the better of him. So, he didn't even use the computer for emails for several years. That meant having me type while he dictated, and then I sent them for him. I didn't enjoy that inconvenience, but he asked for it for the sake of our relationship.

- **Seek counseling.** If you're struggling to take the first step in building trust, a counselor can help you get going and stay on track.

> It's way too easy to stumble on inappropriate images on social media. Seriously. I can't figure out which is a link to a cool motorcycle and which will pop up an inappropriate photo. I need to give Michelle every reason to trust me, so that means being honest about temptation and giving her open access to all of my emails, messages, and browsing history. —*Phil*

The best prayer we can pray is, "Lord, please give me the attitude of Christ toward my spouse. Let us see each other as people who you love. And let us be your agents for loving each other."

We don't always feel warm fuzzies. Sometimes I have to drag my attitude into a better place. I don't naturally let go of a resentment without a battle between my will and God's. I don't naturally let go of an argument without trying to win either. "God, change my attitude" is sometimes the only way I can take a step forward toward what is best for our relationship.

When we forgive, we release our entitlement to win an argument or punish our spouse for a mistake, and we receive the power of God that supercharges our ability to love the other person. When we're married, we no longer search the world over to find true love. If you're still looking for true love, the only place you'll find it is with each other.

> For a lot of years in our earlier marriage, I would half-joke to Michelle about how she would leave me someday for someone smarter and richer. She mentioned often that it bothered her to joke that way, but we finally had a sincere conversation about how it hurt her to imply that lack of trust in her, and I heard what she was saying. She wasn't looking for an upgrade. In the end, it made our relationship stronger to have that conversation, even though I tried to avoid it several times. —*Phil*

Tune-Up Time

- Finish these statements by saying them to each other:

  * I feel genuinely loved when you _____.
  * I feel appreciated when you _____.

- If you think you have drifted apart as a couple, discuss what you think was the starting point of the problem.
- Practice forgiveness. Take turns sharing one wrong from your spouse that you have found it hard to forgive and that keeps you from freely expressing your love. This is something that is not yet resolved, and not something you have already worked through and forgiven.

  * As your partner shares, listen without giving excuses.
  * After your partner shares, give a short statement that acknowledges how your actions hurt them. Again, without excuses or making them feel to blame. Use a statement such as, "I did _____, and that caused you to feel _____."
  * Give an apology that doesn't contain any "if" statements such as, "if I hurt you," or "if you feel this way." Instead, take ownership for the hurt that is real and ask for forgiveness with sincerity. Example: "I apologize for not being truthful about where I was going, and I acknowledge that it violated our trust and caused pain to you, damaging our relationship. Will you forgive me for my wrong?"

* Follow up your spouse's request for forgiveness with a statement that says something like, "I receive your apology and I forgive you. I release you from blame and won't hold this against you, and I choose to pursue restoration and love in our relationship.

- If you are working at building back trust in your relationship, identify which step from this chapter in the section titled "Building Trust and Love" would be an appropriate next step for you as a couple:

    * Commit to break off the affair.
    * Devote yourselves to repentance, forgiving, and rebuilding.
    * Earn back trust.
    * Be honest with each other.
    * Sacrifice.
    * Seek counseling.

Chapter Sixteen

ONE PLUS ONE EQUALS ONE

*W*hen we got married, we filled out some paperwork and then brought it to the county clerk at the courthouse along with our birth certificates. They issued a marriage license, even though we looked like children. On the day of our wedding, we signed the license, our witnesses and Pastor Larry signed it, and then the papers went back to the courthouse to register our marriage. It was a relatively easy process on paper.

When we purchased our current home, we filled out pages and pages of documents. We signed our names fifteen times, or something like that. Maybe it was one hundred. That was all after we had a home inspection, septic inspection, signed an offer to purchase, had a credit report run, and notified our insurance company. Purchasing a home with a thirty-year

> I was twenty-three when we got married. I was a "young twenty-three," which translates as, "I was about as mature as a seventh-grader." —*Phil*

loan is way more extensive than the legal process of getting married. I think we're too flippant about marriage. We see it as a piece of paper and nothing more because it's easy to get married. Before I hop onto a soapbox here, let's look at an illustration I've used with teens that I've mentored in the past.

Try It Before You Buy It

More than once a classmate, coworker, or friend has insisted that it isn't possible to have a good relationship with a potential spouse unless you've lived together or at least had sex before you get engaged. "You wouldn't buy a car without test driving it, would you?" is the silly argument someone will give.

I say it's silly because I think marriage is way more like signing a mortgage than buying a car. When was the last time you got to sleep in a house before you bought it? A home is a big purchase with a long commitment. It isn't like buying a car that wears out in a decade. A house purchase is a long-term commitment, yet we sign a mortgage and transfer a deed before we are allowed to occupy the home. We don't get a trial run with a house. We trust that after careful consideration, it is the home for us. We commit to pay the bank for it and sign the papers; this is our binding promise to fulfill our obligation to pay the mortgage, taxes, and insurance. We know there will be unexpected troubles—all homes have them.

The drain trap under the bathroom sink is going to leak and disgusting water will seep into the floorboards under the vanity. The furnace will quit working on the coldest day in February. The garage door will wedge itself in a position where neither up or down is possible, and you'll be late for work. But in good faith, we know we can fix the problems as they come up.

So, where did this idea come from that makes us think we need to try a bunch of semi-permanent arrangements before we commit to one life-long partner? Dating is our opportunity to weed out the ones that have no possibility as spouse material. And when we believe we have found "the one" we could commit to, we take a step and make a promise that we'll honor our commitment, no matter what comes along. Or that's how God intended it to be.

But when fear enters the picture, we waver and wonder if there is enough trust to build a real relationship. So, we think if we pretend to be married for a while, then we'll know if we're compatible. The problem is, we establish that kind of a relationship on the foundation and belief that there is always an "out." With that kind of thinking, even exchanging rings and signing a paper doesn't fully wipe away the idea that we can walk away if something goes wrong with a "practice" marriage that had no commitment.

There is science to back this up, but right now, I want to speak to your emotions. How secure do you feel if you are always one mistake from breaking up? How confident do you feel if divorce is always an option?

If you went with the try-before-you-buy system of marriage, stay with me here. It isn't my goal to judge or point fingers. Not at all! And it doesn't mean

> Sometimes the other person can't see the problem in the marriage. That reminds me of the time when Michelle told me her transmission was "making a noise," and I responded with, "I don't hear it." (Sometimes she hears things I don't notice.)
>
> Days later when the check engine light was on and she was stranded by the side of road, I got a desperate call with some not-so-friendly words from her. I've learned to listen when she says she hears something in the engine.
>
> Listen when your spouse thinks your marriage needs a repair too. –*Phil*

your marriage is doomed. How you grow your relationship going forward matters more than anything you can't go back and undo.

What Is a Covenant?

A covenant is a contract or legal agreement. But in a biblical sense it is more than that. It is a bond, a personal relationship and not just a signature. When Phil and I got married, going to the courthouse for the documents was easy. But our marriage is a bond, not merely a piece of paper; so, there is more at stake than tearing up a paper if we decide to separate.

Think about what a true bond is. If super glue has a good bond, you shouldn't be able to separate two glued objects from one another without tearing up both surfaces. If my floor tile has a good bond, it won't come up again without smashing it and breaking it apart. I can tear up a piece of paper—a contract—but I cannot break a covenant without smashing both of us.

> That reminds me of the time when we tried to remove that ugly wallpaper on the bedroom wall. That glue was amazing. *—Phil*

With a paper contract—a marriage license—the signatures of two witnesses are enough to make it legally binding. That's required by the state in which you live. But with a covenant, God is the witness, and this is the bond he requires. We make our promise by stating our vows to each other in his presence, and the agreement includes him. That doesn't have to take place in a church, lest you think I'm advocating for that. No. God's Word says that wherever two or three people are gathered together in his name, he is there (that's from Matthew 18:20).

There's a picture of what a covenant marriage looks like in the Bible. A side note here: The Message is a paraphrase of the Bible that puts it into everyday language. I don't recommend a paraphrased Bible for in-depth Bible study—a word-for-word translation is best for that—but sometimes a paraphrase is helpful in pulling the ideas together and providing some additional insight.

This passage has instructions for husbands and wives:

> Out of respect for Christ, be courteously reverent to one another.
>
> Wives, understand and support your husbands in ways that show your support for Christ. The husband provides leadership to his wife the way Christ does to his church, not by domineering but by cherishing. So just as the church submits to Christ as he exercises such leadership, wives should likewise submit to their husbands.
>
> Husbands, go all out in your love for your wives, exactly as Christ did for the church—a love marked by giving, not getting. Christ's love makes the church whole. His words evoke her beauty. Everything he does and says is designed to bring

the best out of her, dressing her in dazzling white silk, radiant with holiness. And that is how husbands ought to love their wives. They're really doing themselves a favor—since they're already "one" in marriage. (Ephesians 5:21–28 The Message)

Mutually submitting to each other. Not one lording it over the other. Not one person demanding anything from the other, but both giving to each other voluntarily. It is the self-sacrificing submission that says, "I will put your needs over my own." If both the husband and the wife do this, both are equally satisfied with the outcome. In a covenant marriage, loving each other means loving Jesus, which is a significant formula in the glue that makes the bond.

Our model for loving each other is based on how Jesus loved us and loved his church enough to give up his life. That's why the church is called the bride of Christ. We—those who follow Christ—are that church, his bride. In a covenant marriage, our love for each other is our ministry to one another in the same way Jesus ministers to the church.

> I have a much better idea now of what a covenant means than I did on the day we were married. Michelle and I both had good examples from our parents of what a covenant marriage was. Our parents were also all married young, and we watched as they went through ups and downs and stayed committed. –*Phil*

If this is starting to sound like a lecture, you need to know that I have a long way to go in getting this right. I'm a work in progress; Phil is a work in progress. We're fellow learners with you. We mess up and apologize and mess up again. We forget each other's needs sometimes and feed our own desires. And then we remember and try again. But understanding our marriage as a covenant instead of a contract keeps our commitment and bond strong, even when we aren't feeling it.

Covenant Is Not Codependency

Mutual submission to one another within the covenant with God in marriage is not the same as being codependent. We are not the center

> When we made that commitment, I was naïve in my thinking about the responsibilities that come along with a covenant. But over the years we have both learned and changed and grown up. Being "one" doesn't mean thinking exactly alike or being clones of each other, but it means that our promise to each other and to God is the cornerstone of our relationship, even when we disagree. *—Phil*

of one another's universe—God is. In God's marriage math, one plus one equals one. The passage from Ephesians goes on to say, "A man leaves his father and mother and is joined to his wife, and the two are united into one" (Ephesians 5:31). Here Paul quotes a verse from Genesis 2:24, which means this has been established since the very first marriage.

Sex is an expression of this unity and not just an act of animal instinct. Within God's plan from the beginning for humans, it is a sacred expression of the covenant.

With marriage math, I'm not one half, and Phil is not another half; this means we are not two halves that finally complete each other. We are each one, complete with God as our leader and creator, and together we are also one—a couple, a unit.

This is why it's so important that each of us has a relationship where Jesus Christ is the head of our life. When each of us is secure in who we are in Christ and what that means for us, then we have a foundation for marriage. If that foundation is lopsided, marriage is going to be more challenging. A lot more challenging.

You might say, "I know just as many people who go to church who get divorced as I know people who don't go to church and get divorced." This is possible. But please also note that not everyone who goes to church has a genuine relationship with Jesus. Some of them like to hang out at God's house, but they haven't yet become part of his family. And of course, some Christians who love Jesus with all of their hearts are divorced; I don't want to paint broad strokes of judgment here.

Not everyone had a choice in the matter. Some have weathered terrible abuse. My heart breaks for marriages that didn't survive.

Child of God

Let's unpack that idea of hanging out at God's house a little more. Over the years, we've had a lot of kids hang out at our house. We have an unusual home that used to be a country church and parsonage. Basically, we have a one-hundred-year-old church attached to our ranch house.

The church sanctuary is a rec room where our boys would have friends over to play video games, play ping-pong, and have slumber parties on old metal army cots. I baked many loaves of bread and fed many jars of homemade strawberry jam to the boys that came over to visit. Some of them even called me mom for baking bread and filling their bellies.

But even though they hung out at my house, none of those kids had the same rights as our boys. They didn't have our last name. They didn't have their own bedroom at our house.

> I restored a classic Jeep for each of my sons but not for their friends. However, there was that time when Michelle wanted to reduce the number of parts vehicles I kept in the back yard and she tried to give those away each time one of the kids had a friend over. You get a Jeep. You get a Jeep. You get a Jeep. –*Phil*

We didn't write them into our will. We didn't write checks for their college tuition or hand them twenty-dollar bills for gas money. But if we had adopted any of them, they would have had the same rights as our biological children.

Some people hang out at God's house every week and call themselves Christians. But not all of them are really children of God. Some are there for the fun of seeing their friends every week. Here's what the Bible tells us to help us know the real children of God:

> But you are not controlled by your sinful nature. You are controlled by the Spirit if you have the Spirit of God living in you. (And remember that those who do not have the Spirit of Christ living in them do not belong to him at all.) And Christ lives within you, so even though your body will die because of sin, the Spirit gives

you life because you have been made right with God. The Spirit of God, who raised Jesus from the dead, lives in you. And just as God raised Christ Jesus from the dead, he will give life to your mortal bodies by this same Spirit living within you.

Therefore, dear brothers and sisters, you have no obligation to do what your sinful nature urges you to do. For if you live by its dictates, you will die. But if through the power of the Spirit you put to death the deeds of your sinful nature, you will live. For all who are led by the Spirit of God are children of God.

So you have not received a spirit that makes you fearful slaves. Instead, you received God's Spirit when he adopted you as his own children. Now we call him, "Abba, Father." For his Spirit joins with our spirit to affirm that we are God's children. And since we are his children, we are his heirs. (Romans 8:9–17)

When we receive pardon from Jesus, we are adopted into God's family. We have the full rights of children. We are no longer visiting at God's house; we are family. We are heirs. Sons and daughters. We have a name.

This is also a covenant. God made a promise that he would send Jesus "to save the world through him" (John 3:17). When we individually enter into the covenant of salvation, it gives new meaning to our marriage covenant. Just as our offspring will carry on our name and our legacy, we carry on the name and legacy of Jesus.

Do you have a name in God's family? If you read that and realized you don't know if you're part of God's family or not, the process isn't difficult. Jesus already paid the price for adoption; all it will cost you is surrender of your pride and your own stubborn will.

When you surrender your pride, you're admitting you can't be perfect enough to deserve forgiveness through your own efforts. You're admitting you need Jesus and you believe his sacrifice on the cross is enough to wipe out all of your wrongs. And you declare you're turning from your own path and surrendering your will to God's will.

When you're part of God's family, your identity in Christ is more significant than your identity as a husband or a wife. It gives your marriage a solid place to weather out what life throws your way. It gives hope when a crisis comes and you don't know what to do.

If you didn't invite God to be part of your marriage on the day of your wedding, you still can. Many couples renew their vows later when they come to a place where they want to make a fresh start after committing to follow Christ. It doesn't have to be a fancy ceremony. It can be a simple prayer between the two of you.

> I don't like to take my truck to a mechanic until I have tried every YouTube video and possible fix myself. Even thought I'm a DIY guy, YouTube isn't going to fix a marriage. Sometimes we need to know when to ask for help. –*Phil*

If you live with regret over a marriage that broke apart, ask God for forgiveness for any role you had in it, and let the shame go. If you're in a second marriage, commit to doing whatever it takes to fulfil that covenant. We can't go back and change the past. We can only learn from it and move forward.

For Phil and me, being in a covenant isn't only about staying together. It also means actively pursuing what would make our marriage healthy. We attend church together, we have friendships with other couples, and we have our own individual friends who are also pursuing healthy marriages.

We study the Bible. We listen to Christian podcasts or read books that help us grow our faith and live like Jesus.

> I suggested that a nice illustration would be that I am like the engine and she is like the tranny (transmission) and both must be working for the whole car to run, but that got an eye-roll. So, we might have a little work of our own to do. –*Phil*

Our prayer for you is that your marriage would thrive and flourish. If your relationship is good enough now, we pray it will grow to become great. If you're overwhelmed and wish you could go back for a do-over, we encourage you to make this your start over.

One plus one equals one. Which of you will make the first move in changing the math for your marriage?

Tune-Up Time

- Watch your wedding video together or go through your photo album together. Describe how you thought about marriage then and what it means to you now.
- Discuss how you think a contract and a covenant are different.

  * Which one do you think best represents how you would describe your marriage right now?
  * How could you commit or recommit to your covenant with one another and with God?

- Read your wedding vows to one another or talk out the details for planning a small ceremony to renew your commitment.
- Take turns describing where you would like to see your relationship in five years, ten years, and twenty years from now.
- Do you agree or disagree with this statement? Our relationship is solid on the foundation of our shared faith in Jesus Christ.

  * Explain why you agree or disagree.
  * What would you like to change in your relationship if you disagree with the statement right now?
  * Discuss and come to an agreement on what your next step will be regarding growing your foundation in Jesus Christ.

Future

Chapter Seventeen

MORE GIVE AND LESS TAKE

Is it possible to change one's anniversary date? I've often wondered if getting married between Christmas and New Year's was such a great idea. Not because of the busyness of the holidays and the difficulty in squeezing in an anniversary meal or a get-away, although that is a hurdle to be reckoned with; it's because of something I hadn't anticipated. Hunting.

Phil is an avid hunter, but during our dating years and for the first few years of marriage, he wasn't all that into the sport. At first, he was more into spending time with me. Isn't that precious. But as time went by, the call of the wild drew him to the woods as my wild calls for help in the kitchen drove him to seek solitude in a tree stand.

I can't say I blame him, but the timing of hunting season has caused its share of strife in our marriage. He would often spend most of his Thanksgiving in the woods with a rifle across his lap while I mashed potatoes and basted turkey with the other women. He'd come in for dinner and a nap; for safety reasons, he wouldn't return to the woods until the turkey coma wore off.

Rifle hunting is a weeklong season that I've learned to deal with because it puts meat on the table, at least sometimes. Mostly, it makes him happy, and I like that.

Taking Stock in Patience

A week of rifle hunting is one thing, but bow season is another story. For years, the bow season in our state ran from the middle of September to New Year's Eve—the whole fourth quarter of the year and then some! Often while I was putting an evergreen in a Christmas tree stand, he was still dreaming of sitting up in his tree stand looking for antlers.

One would think three and a half months is plenty of time for a man to find a deer and shoot it, but a real bow hunter doesn't shoot his buck until he is sure he has found the biggest trophy possible. This means he passes up some great deer. It also means that by the last week of December, Phil is pretty desperate to shoot something. Fresh snow is perfect for tracking deer; so, this adds to the attraction of hunting in December, especially on Christmas Eve, Christmas Day, and all the days leading up to New Year's—including our anniversary.

> Over time, my obsession with hunting has been replaced by my obsession with restoring Jeeps. We've had some of the same conversations about the amount of time I spend at the shop working on cars as we once did about the time I spent hunting for deer.
>
> To be fair, Michelle sometimes snuggles up with her laptop more than she snuggles up with me–she loves writing and graphic design as much as I like engines and antlers. –*Phil*

"I'm not going to shoot anything. I'm purely going out to look," he'd promise.

"What's the point, then?" I'd argue.

"Well, just in case."

"So, if the biggest buck of your life walked by, you'd shoot?"

"Maybe."

"Then you're not just looking, you're hunting," I'd sigh.

He'd put on the camouflage and kiss me goodbye, his eyes pleading for me to understand.

Ammunition for Conflict

One anniversary, he did see the perfect eight-point buck, which is how I ended up dressed to the nines, smelling like a cherry blossom, and seething over his absence at the hour we were supposed to be heading out for a candlelit dinner. When he came in from the woods, I met him with folded arms and gave him the evil eye—the look that scares him more than his mother ever did when he was in trouble. I recognized the victory in his eyes. Or maybe it was in the silly grin on his face.

"I'm sorry, Hon. Mmm, you look nice. Hey, I got the biggest buck I've ever shot, and I have to go out and track him. We'll go out when I get back."

He called his best hunting buddy for help tracking—and for mutual celebrating, since I wasn't in the celebrating mood.

> My sitting in a tree stand just to look for deer is pretty much the same as my wife going into Target just to look. "I'm not going to buy anything" and "I'm not going to shoot anything" are pretty much equal statements.
>
> Plus, I have a nice head mount to show for it. You don't see the perfect pair of leggings and a sweater hanging on our wall, but there is some pretty sweet taxidermy on display there. —*Phil*

Giving Peace a Shot

Thanks to a skilled taxidermist, that deer hangs on our wall, surrounded by two other nearly identical eight-point bucks, at least one of which is from another late December hunt. Funny thing is, I can't remember if we went out to eat that night. I remember having words about the timing of his victory, but I know we made up. We always do. That's the point of promising in good times and in bad times in our wedding vows.

There are going to be times when our spouse really ticks us off. And there are going to be times when we don't handle our conflicts all that well. But marriage is about the give and take, and sometimes we have to learn the hard way how to give a little more and take a lot less. I'm in a forever learning process about how not to make a big deal about some things; he's forever learning how to consider my feelings. We can learn to respect our spouses for their uniqueness and to be considerate of the things that bring them joy, but it takes work—some give and take.

I'm glad I can't remember all of our conflicts. As we look forward to another anniversary, I have no regrets about marrying my husband, hunting and all. I'll keep forgiving him for his love of the outdoors and I'll keep cooking the meat he brings home for the table. And I'm thankful that we don't have to change our December anniversary, since bow season has been extended into January now—making it last for a full one-third of every year.

> I would give up my hobbies in a heartbeat if it meant saving my marriage, but I don't want to be so unaware of our relationship that I wait until it's too late to make a change. We talk often about Michelle's desire to spend more time with me.
>
> I have suggested that we spend some quality time hanging out while I weld a frame on a truck or replace a transmission, but apparently that isn't what she's asking for.
>
> All kidding aside, I want to meet that need in a way that helps her to know I value our time together. *–Phil*

Learning How to Give

My first inclination in marriage conflicts is not giving. I'm a natural taker. I want to win. I'm not proud of that quality. Let's be real here; even the most selfless among us have "me" moments. That's because deep within us is something the Bible calls a sin nature. We have a natural bent toward pleasing ourselves, meeting our desires, getting things our way, and listening to our feelings. It takes training to stop and ask it to be quiet for a moment when the me-centered nature is shouting. That's when our other-centered nature whispers things such as, "He didn't do it on purpose." Or, "Let's give him the benefit of the doubt."

Then, right there, the two voices have a little shouting match within my heart, and I have to choose which one to listen to. Sometimes other-centered wins. Sometimes I have a pouting party and throw a little tantrum. Eventually I settle down and shame takes over. In the end, it's grace that wins. I receive God's grace when I ask for forgiveness, and Phil extends grace to me as I learn one more lesson about how to use my inside voice. Yes, I shout when I'm mad. I think it's better when the whole neighborhood knows our business. No. Not really. Mostly it's that I get passionately worked up when my me-centered nature acts like my boss.

If you get worked up about things, then you understand the inner battle. You understand the process of learning how to have healthy reactions to conflicts, rather than harmful ones.

> Michelle has compromised too. For example, I spent our thirtieth anniversary at the shop helping our son Austin with a big Jeep project because it was Christmas break and he was off from teaching school. She understood that the timing of it was our only window of opportunity, so we agreed to go out for our celebration dinner a few days later.
>
> There are other times when I know it's right for me to set aside time to spend time with Michelle or family, even when I have a big car project that I wish I could finish.
>
> One year I even skipped deer hunting so we could take a family vacation. –*Phil*

Giving Up

If marriage is a give-and-take relationship, then part of it is shifting from a mindset where we try to give and take equally to where we focus on giving more than taking. It also changes what it means to give up. Instead of giving up on our marriage, we give up on the self-focus that could destroy our relationship. Here are some examples of what we've worked on giving up in our marriage:

Give up being right. How often do you find yourself arguing, correcting, or saying, "I told you so"? Does it really make you happy if your spouse gives up and lets you be right? This might come as a shocker, but it's rare that a conversation ends this way: "Thank you so much for hammering that home. I can't believe how wrong I was. Good thing I have you to point out my failures and mistakes."

It usually goes more like this: "Fine. You win." This is said to make you go away, not to admit victory. It really means, "I'll say anything to make this stop."

The real factor at work here isn't being right. It is being prideful. Pride is what makes us want to look good, even if it means making someone else look bad.

> Are you reading my sarcastic thoughts again? —*Phil*

Give up expecting perfection. If you have a framed picture in your mind of what the perfect marriage looks like, it probably has to do with what you expect from your spouse. Toss it out. Your mind needs a new wall hanging. Jesus gave us this picture, "There is no greater love than to lay down one's life for one's friends" (John 15:13). This is perfect, sacrificial love.

A perfect marriage isn't romantic gestures, vacations, roses, sex every day, or having all of your needs met. Your expectations will set you up for disappointment as you spend your days waiting for your spouse to meet them, only to feel frustrated at the end of every stinkin' day. Instead, if you aim for serving the other person, you might be surprised to discover how much closer your relationship becomes.

Give up comparing to others. Very little good comes from comparing your marriage to someone else's. First, if theirs is great and yours is floundering, it can lead to resentment and discouragement. Unless you compare to your grandparents who have been married for seventy-five years and find inspiration in their example, most comparison is a trap. Even seventy-five-year marriages aren't perfect.

If you compare with another couple who have been married about the same amount of time as you, there is the possibility that you'll note something they have that is missing in your spouse. You might notice something missing in you, too, but we're way more likely to go after change in our spouse than we are in ourselves. And if you compare and find your marriage to be better, there is a danger of either becoming prideful or becoming complacent. It leads to statements that begin with, "At least we don't..." That pattern of thinking leads to settling for good enough instead of great.

Give up complaining about your spouse. I have a couple of close girlfriends who I reach out to for accountability and prayer. I'm careful about what I share with even them. I refuse to sit around in a circle of friends and make it a complaining session about our husbands. When we do share, we're careful to discuss how we can pray for each other, and we pray that we would be changed too. We pray that we would have gracious and loving attitudes and respond in a way that leads to healing and resolution.

We don't vent to each other and whine about how terrible our husbands are. Guys, we ask this of you, too. If your wife has gained a few pounds and you've noticed, don't shame her in front of your friends. And if her sexual desire has changed, patiently help her to feel loved and secure, rather than airing that info to some guys over a few beers. Unless our friends hold us accountable for how we react to our spouse's shortcomings, nothing good will come from venting our frustrations to them.

Give up expecting the worst. As I'm explaining something to him, Phil will sometimes fill in the story before he knows the details. I'm guilty of it too. We often assume we know what the other person is thinking. While our spouse is in the process of explaining, we might anticipate the worst and already start to create a defense in our heads to a problem that doesn't exist.

For example, when Phil and I talked through some old issues when we participated in the marriage class at church, we discovered that Phil still

> My grandparents did argue plenty over their seventy-five years of marriage. As their hearing started to go, there were many times they weren't even arguing about the same thing. But they kept a sense of humor.
>
> There was that time when they were both well into their nineties and they were sorting out their pills before a holiday meal with family, and with a gleam in his eye, Grandpa leaned over to ask Grandma, "You rememberin' to take your birth control pills, Marion?"
>
> That was for the benefit of getting a laugh from the grandchildren who were within hearing.
>
> Grandma gave her usual response to his pranks, "Oh Fred." –*Phil*

assumed—despite my assurances—if I wasn't in the mood for intimacy, it was because I was repulsed by him.

I had to continue to assure him that it had everything to do with my hormone cycles, my level of exhaustion, and my disappointment with my body size. Sometimes it seemed like so much effort to get past all of those factors. It had nothing to do with what I thought of him at that moment.

> Michelle is very direct, which means we work out our differences together and I'm not tried in the court of opinion of her friends and family. I appreciate that, even as a conflict avoider. —*Phil*

When he perceived I was repulsed by him, he withdrew and sulked. This added a new factor to my struggle, and I didn't know what to do with it. But when he understood the internal battle I was having, he relaxed and treated me with gentle compassion. That reassured me and eased some of the stress. And surprisingly, it removes some of the inhibitions when the tension is lessened.

Guys, this doesn't mean it's a give and take that works this way: you act nice and compassionate, and she'll make love to you. Okay? It isn't a formula like that. It isn't fake compassion. It takes patient understanding on both sides. You don't always get the results you want right at the moment. Your motive has to be about loving your spouse without expecting anything in return.

And women, put yourself in his shoes. If he feels rejected and doesn't understand how you're really feeling, help him to connect with your pain without pushing him away. Ask to simply be together, with no strings attached, so you can feel his presence and appreciate his closeness and support. Assure him that you need his kindness and compassion to help you through this inner turmoil. Teach him how there is more to physical touch than just foreplay.

Giving up expecting the worst applies to so many areas of conflict in a marriage. When Phil calls me and says, "Now hear me out . . . During my lunch break, I was browsing on Facebook Marketplace . . . ," I have to listen without verbally attacking. That is, oh, so difficult sometimes. Based on past experience, I know this probably means he is about to withdraw cash from the ATM and drive into the next state to purchase parts for his truck. "Parts" come with axles and tires attached to them at our house. This means he's about to make a case for purchasing a clunker to park in our back yard and from which he will strip parts from now until infinity, or until he needs more "parts."

There was a time when we were up to nine Jeeps out back. Nine. They were behind a fence, but they were well documented by Google Earth. Phil has a valid reason for his method, and over the years, he's saved us a lot of money doing self-repairs, so I keep practicing my patience.

> Who is counting? Hear me out here. I was thinking of getting this Jeep Comanche. It has a really good topper on it, and I need a topper for my other Comanche. —*Phil*

Give up feeling sorry for yourself. If your marriage isn't what you'd like right now, you aren't going to feel better if you bury yourself in self-pity. Do anything but that. Decide on what you can do, even if your marriage has lost its luster. Look for the glimmers of hope that shine through the dull moments and appreciate each laugh you have together. Pour your energy into praying for your spouse and showing unconditional love. If you're in an abusive relationship, this does not apply. There are appropriate times to seek professional counsel and remove yourself from an unsafe situation, whether that is physically unsafe or emotionally unsafe. I'm talking to those of us who feel sorry for ourselves when we have given up on a perfectly salvageable marriage.

Taking Charge of Change

Change begins with me. I can't change my husband, even though I have foolishly acted as if it were my job to change him for the past thirty-plus years. I can change myself—my reactions, my thoughts, my actions. It doesn't happen right away. Sometimes it is gradual. But every step matters.

I like illustrations that help me understand a concept, so this one might create a helpful picture of how it works. Piano strings are sort of like heavy-duty and extra-large guitar strings. They're hidden away inside the piano body, but a professional tuner has a key that fits on their pegs, which he can turn to tighten each string and make it sound the right tone. The more out of tune the instrument is, the more cranking is required on those strings. Tuning is important because the only way a piano can accompany another instrument is if they are both correctly tuned.

> I don't know much about musical instruments at all, but my siblings took lessons when we had an old upright piano that stood in the room off the kitchen in my childhood home. That piano definitely needed some tuning. –*Phil*

However, when a piano is way out of tune, the tuner does not tighten the stings all the way at once. He tightens them to work in harmony with one another, even if they aren't yet at the correct pitch. Then, at the next tuning he will tighten them more. Eventually, everything will be perfectly tuned. If he tunes them all to the correct pitch in the first session, the strings will break.

As we tune our marriage, it has to be gradual. Very rarely does a marriage go from out of tune to perfect harmony overnight. A little give here, and less take there will lead to a pleasant melody with time. As my heart is tuned to God's will for a wife, Phil's is tuned to God's will for a husband. And eventually, the two make nice music.

We also need to tune our marriage before we can make beautiful music in other relationships. Similar to how a piano can't play in harmony with another instrument until it's tuned to the correct pitch, our number one priority has to be our marriage—tuned first to God and each other. Then we'll be tuned to the correct pitch to work with others. This might mean stepping back from some outside distractions to wholeheartedly focus on getting our marriage in a better place. It might mean giving up hunting for one season, or giving up volunteering on the PTA. It could mean replacing separate evenings out with guy or girl friends and having couple time instead.

I'm grateful that Phil has been willing to work on staying in tune with God and with me. I'm thankful that he puts up with this bossy and sassy gal as we both learn how to assume the best, overlook each other's imperfections, and live in harmony.

Tune-Up Time

- Discuss the difference between each of you giving 50 percent and taking 50 percent versus each of you giving 100 percent in your relationship.

    * What do you think it would change in your marriage if you both adopted the 100-percent mindset?

- Name one area in your relationship where you feel like you're a taker and could become more of a giver.
- Of the list of things to give up in this chapter, which one resonates most with you?

    * Give up being right.
    * Give up expecting perfection.
    * Give up comparing to others.
    * Give up complaining about your spouse.
    * Give up expecting the worst.
    * Give up feeling sorry for yourself.

- Discuss where you think your relationship is in regard to being in tune with each other. On a scale of 1–10, how would you rate your current state of unity as a couple, where one is the least in tune and ten is the most in tune?

    * What do you think causes the most disharmony between you?
    * Discuss together what your next step will be to work on harmony with each other.

- Take a few minutes to each create a list of five ways you could be more giving to your spouse. Then read your lists to each other. (This exercise is about focusing completely on how you can be more giving *for* each other, versus asking for something *from* each other.)
- Finish your discussion by sharing two or three ways your spouse is generous with their giving to you and express appreciation for that.

Chapter Eighteen

FOR BETTER OR FOR HEARSE

Have you ever received a text message from your husband when you were out on a special day with your girlfriends and he wanted to know where the ketchup was? It goes something like this:

Hey babe. We out of ketchup?

No. Why?

There isn't any in the fridge.

Yes there is.

Nope. Looked.

It's on the middle shelf, next to the milk. Red bottle with Heinz on the front.

Looked there.

By the maple syrup?

Nope.

K. I'll buy some.

You bring home ketchup and put it in the refrigerator—right next to the bottle you told him was there. On the middle shelf, next to the milk. There's another one by the syrup.

To write a large portion of this book, I checked myself into a retreat center for five days with limited cell service and spotty internet. I unplugged to focus and withdraw from everyday distractions, but while I there, the following message from Phil came through.

> My eyesight really isn't what it used to be. –*Phil*

We hadn't used the DVD player in months, but he was having his buddy Jack over to watch a movie while I was away, so this constituted an emergency, I guess:

Can you tell me what source on the TV I'm supposed to use to make the DVD player work?

AV

I tried that.

It's already plugged in on the back of the TV, right? I think I remember a cord coming off the TV. Otherwise, Dallas is the person to ask.

Ok that's what I have it on. Plugged in but get nothing.

> DVD player needs to be on
> the right thing too.

Yeah it says DVD player. Not sure what to do next. I could always purchase Jeremiah Johnson on Prime Video for $3.50.

> Please call Dallas. DVD
> player works fine.

Meanwhile, I texted our son, Dallas, and asked him to talk to Dad. Dallas lived two hours away from home, but when he lived at home, he had a whole system for how he hooked up old players to our smart TV.

Pause. No response from either guy.

At last a ding.

Dallas got it going for me.

> I knew he would.

I figured he was trying to provide me with extra writing material. So, here you go. There will be times when getting a DVD player working will constitute an emergency worth interrupting your personal time. There will be a hundred times when you have to get out of your chair to locate something in the cupboard that is perfectly aligned with your guy's eyeballs, but he can't see it.

Imagine if the shoe were on the other foot and you couldn't get Hallmark Channel to work. Wait. I guess you wouldn't call me. Okay. Imagine that the car wouldn't start, and you were getting ready to go out for coffee with friends. —*Phil*

There will be times when I leave dirty coffee cups in the sink and he'll put them in the dishwasher. Okay. Lots of times. He'll soak petrified fried egg off a plate because I ate a hasty breakfast before taking the three steps up the hall to my office and left the plate on the counter. He'll help me turn vintage items into treasures and then watch me sell his hard work on Facebook Marketplace. He'll listen to me explain the ins and outs of social media advertising and changes to the algorithm until his eyes glaze over, even though he has no idea what I'm talking about. "Algo-what?"

Forever Is Our Future

I take you . . . to have and to hold
from this day forward;
for better or for worse,
for richer, for poorer,
in sickness and in health,
to love and to cherish,
until death us do part.

> I remind myself often that Michelle isn't only in my life for scheduling online bills, being my personal IT person for when my phone stops working, or my secretary who schedules appointments and family gatherings. She is my best friend. Losing her wouldn't be about losing what she takes care of for me but about losing part of who I am. I don't want to take her for granted. —*Phil*

In comparison with many of our loved ones and friends, our vows have hardly been tested. For better or for worse . . . until death do us part really means "for better or for hearse." That covers everything in between.

We stick it out in the good times and in the bad ones, until one of us leaves this earth. It sounds easy when we're standing in front of a preacher and 250 of our family and friends in an over-decorated venue on a Saturday afternoon. But when it comes down to crisis, illness, discouragement, disappointment, and even betrayal, the situation is multilayered, complicated, and like navigating through land mines.

There will be times when you would rather give up. But you won't. You'll say ugly, hurtful things to each other and wish you could retract them, but you can't. You won't want to be nice or do something sacrificial for the other person, but you will.

Our sickness and health promise has not given us much practice. A flu bug here and there, a knee surgery, wisdom teeth, back troubles, one wily appendix, childbirth—nothing all that serious. But in the last year, we had a glimpse of the humility and grace that some people experience on a grander scale. Around age fifty, Phil's prostate decided it needed to do some bodybuilding and he experienced benign prostatic hyperplasia (BPH). Also called prostate enlargement, this is a noncancerous increase in the size of the prostate gland.

At first, it meant waking up often in the night to use the restroom, then frequent stops at every store, gas station, and restaurant restroom whenever we were out, and eventually a significant problem with "going" at all. This also proved that his bladder was up to Olympic medal status for its ability to retain liquid.

> Suddenly, Michelle was the one who was waiting for me in the hallway whenever we stopped at a public restroom instead of the other way around—me waiting for her. She could even fix her hair and put on lipstick and still get out of there faster. —*Phil*

The doctor emphasized that Phil had an exceptionally large—let's say, overachieving—prostate for a man of his age, and he would need surgery to reduce it. We'd hoped he would be in and out of the outpatient surgery center and home by mid-afternoon as planned. But he doesn't come out of anesthesia well and has frequent vomiting until it wears off after sixteen hours or so. I've never been someone who does well with vomiting, even though I was once a hospital nurse. Yet by the grace of God, I was able to hold his plastic barf bag for him throughout that day with not one gag from me. I even held it while sipping on a Frappuccino with the other hand. Once they admitted him to the hospital for overnight observation, I drove home to rest.

He came home the next day with a urinary catheter that was to remain in place for four days. We had a lot of firsts over that weekend. I emptied his urine bag, helped him shower and put on fresh pajamas, helped him out of the chair and walked beside him when he was woozy, and I forced him to drink the giant tumblers of liquid that the doctor ordered. For well over a month after surgery, Phil experienced bleeding any time he was too

Yeesh. This memory gives me the heebie-jeebies. Michelle was an excellent nurse, but if I ever misbehave, all anyone has to do is threaten me with a plastic tube the size of a garden hose. No. No. No way Jose. —*Phil*

active. For a man who is extremely active—hyper sometimes—a lifting and activity restriction is like prison. We were both thankful when he was fully healed, and, praise God, the surgery was successful.

This was a bonding experience for us, but it also gave us a new appreciation for those who are full-time caregivers for a spouse. Marriage vows mean nothing until they are truly proven through action.

As Long as We Both Shall Live

When we say marriage is forever, we mean it's for the span of our lifetime, which at the age of twenty, sounded like an eternity to me. At age fifty, it still does! When we say forever, we really mean for our entire future, however long that is. There's only one little problem. The length of that span of time is completely out of our hands.

My mom and dad have celebrated fifty-two anniversaries and counting. My mom had cancer when they had been married for twenty-eight years. She is a survivor. Phil's parents had forty-three years together before cancer took his mom's life. "Forever" has different numbers.

For Phil's grandparents, for better or for worse included farming, retirement, senior apartment, assisted living, and finally a nursing home. They had spunk! Grandma Rayburn wouldn't go to the nursing home unless it had high-speed internet so she could continue playing solitaire online—in her mid-nineties.

The older we get, the more I realize our time together is limited. My mom had recently retired when the cancer diagnosis came. They had plans for retirement together. Too often I think of someday instead of today, and I think, "Someday when I have more time, I'll spend more of it with Michelle." But someday might not come, and I could be left with regret. It's a wake-up call for today. —*Phil*

One of my grandmothers passed away when I was a freshman in college. My grandpa remarried one of her dear friends the same year Phil and I got married. They had twenty-two years together before she died.

One of our friends was a widow at thirty-nine when her husband's sudden death left her with four young children to raise. They certainly expected more than thirteen years of marriage together. That changed overnight.

My aunt passed away after a short flu illness at the age of fifty-one. In one weekend, their future stopped.

I share these stories to underscore that every day is a gift. Sometimes I look across the room and wonder if I can handle thirty more years of his snoring in the recliner with the remote in hand. He probably wonders if he can handle another thirty years of my phobia of smacking and chewing noises—that will probably get worse if he ever needs dentures! But then we remember that our time together is a gift.

This chapter is about living, not about dying. It's about living with no regrets. No wife stands next to the grave of her loving husband and says, "I showed too much kindness to him." No man buries his wife and says, "I showed her that I cherished her too much." We say all sorts of wonderful things about them in a eulogy; why not say those things when they are living?

> This whole topic sounds depressing. I don't like to deal with reality sometimes because it gets into emotions I'm better at stuffing. But time is a gift, and I don't want to be so busy, or complacent, or stubborn that I don't appreciate that gift *—Phil*

Living the Eulogy

In a for-better-or-for-hearse marriage, the key is learning how to create our eulogy as we live it. If we want to be known as loving, caring, giving, or self-sacrificing, we have to be those things. Let's make it easy to write a eulogy because we have more than enough wonderful things to say about each other. Typically, we want kindness and tenderness from our spouse, but we don't want to be humble enough to show it to them as well. So, it takes practice to live other-focused. I want to share with you some of the things that have gotten in our way and some of our observations about other marriages; maybe you can find inspiration to strengthen your own relationship for better or for hearse.

Pride – Over the course of thirty years, I have had plenty of moments where I wanted to do the nice thing. I wanted to apologize. I wanted to make the first move. But I didn't want it bad enough to set aside my pride to follow through with action. Every time, it was an opportunity lost.

Pride is a liar. It looks like a shell that would protect a vulnerable heart from getting hurt, but instead it extends the hurt and blocks healing. It puts my own self over the other person. It manifests itself with unkind words and silent treatments.

Stubbornness – This is pride's cousin. Stubbornness blocks many mediocre marriages from becoming magnificent. If they could only say they're sorry. If only they could set aside their preferences and make an exception. Stubbornness includes holding on to the legalistic idea that caring for the children is all her responsibility or mowing the grass is all his—and then suddenly one of you is gone. Then you wonder if maybe that wasn't worth taking your last stand on.

Is it worth watching your TV show while she struggles to give a bath to three kids? Is it worth it to insist she waits on you and brings you a beer, even if she's exhausted and looks as though she could use a massage? Is it worth nagging him to make the appointment to get the oil changed when it's a two-minute call at the most, and you'll be the one taking the minivan in anyway? Is it worth refusing to have a conversation about the possibility of his changing jobs and your moving to a different neighborhood so he can have less stress and be a better father and husband? You love your house and your friends, but is it worth watching him die a little bit every day that he goes to work?

Stubbornness is a liar too. We believe our needs are so important that it's worth holding our ground to protect them, but it blocks us from seeing the consequences of our actions or caring about them. Getting past pride and stubbornness takes humility. It means learning to be self-aware and admitting to our own flaws.

Busyness – If Satan had one tool that could ruin all marriages, this is the pyramid scheme of all pyramid schemes. If you're too busy, so are most of your friends because you're all interconnected with your plans and programs. You're in the PTA together, in the softball league, at the soccer games, volunteering at the library, joining a neighborhood club, serving on every committee, bringing kids to ballet and violin lessons, enrolling them in the summer science program at the park, and on it goes. If your friends' kids do it, you believe yours should too. So, one household at a time, schedules become more and more packed.

> I have had three jobs in the thirty years we have been married. Michelle was supportive every time I was ready for a career change.
>
> Twice my job change involved a move to a different home. She has adapted to leaving friends and family, living in a new neighborhood, income fluctuations, and seeing me less during some of these moves.
>
> We've had some normal conflict as we both adapted, but we have both learned to give and take and work through the struggles. –*Phil*

It isn't only parents who experience this. As an empty nester, I know it too. Now we have all this "free" time, so empty nesters volunteer at church, take that art class we always wanted to take, go back to school, join a golf league, buy a second home and spend weekends mowing grass at two places, become the daycare provider for our grandkids, and more.

Busyness puts us on the verge of a breakdown and wears out our patience for each other. We use it all up with our activities, so when we get home, we let our hair down—or put our hair up in a messy bun—and let each other have the worst of what we have left. This is not what for better or for worse means. It was not for "worse" that we were created.

We couldn't have seen it coming when we started writing this book, but when the COVID-19 pandemic hit in the spring of 2020 and businesses and activities had to shut down for more than two months, it was almost a relief to let go of busyness because we had to. It gave us the opportunity to practice doing less because we had the governor's permission to stay home.

But we don't need an order from the governor to change our schedules! For the sake of our mental health and relationships, we can say no to activities, even without a pandemic.

Complacency – Do you take your spouse for granted? Do you do the same thing day in and day out and assume he or she is happy with good enough? Complacency is not the same as contentment. It happens when we think we've done all the work we need to do for our marriage, and then we coast. It means we settle. After a while, it could lead to a decision that we've had enough with good enough, which will either lead to change or divorce.

The message complacency sends is, "We don't care." It starts with, "I don't care," but if neither of us does anything about that, it becomes a "we" problem. We are both responsible for our relationship. I think back to when Phil and I were dating and I couldn't wait to see him again. We used to sit together on the one loveseat we owned. That was before we purchased recliners and had our own spaces. Sometimes, getting past complacency is as simple as doing something you used to do—like sitting on the couch together. Other times it is changing things up and doing something new together. Compliment each other and point out each other's strengths and talents. Talk about your dreams for the future and how you can fulfill those dreams together.

> I was looking around our house the other day and noticed the creative ways Michelle has fixed something or repurposed a junk-find as a decoration. I paused to tell her I appreciate her creativity. I want to be more aware of opportunities to encourage her and tell her I'm proud of her now instead of saying it someday in her eulogy. Especially because she is a better writer than I am. She will write something creative about me. *–Phil*

Laziness – Remember when you said please and thank you to each other? We get lazy in our relationships! When was the last time you said, "I love you"? I have heard couples say that love is assumed in their relationship and they don't need to say it. They believe doing their duties of going to work or cooking a meal are enough to send the message that they love each other. I disagree. I'm not promoting the idea of saying it flippantly just to say it; but look for opportunities to say it and mean it. Maybe you need to write it out in a love note to leave in his jacket, or on the mirror for her to find when she wakes up. Dry erase markers work great on a mirror!

Did you once make his coffee for him in the morning, but now he makes it himself? Surprise him with a cup again. Was there a time when you held the door for your wife, but you can't remember when that stopped? Surprise her and try it again. Listen again. Wake up your feelings for each other. Kiss again. Kiss longer—this would be Phil's advice. Invite passion back into your marriage. Invite Jesus back into your marriage.

ᴄ⁊

If you aren't dead, you aren't done. Someday, one of you will watch the other one be driven away in a hearse. This is your wakeup call to live now. If you're still married, your relationship isn't dead either. You aren't done improving your marriage. You aren't done learning how to love like Jesus loves. Live in such a way that later, you can say, "We loved well."

Tune-Up Time

- If you could write something funny for your own headstone, what would you want it to say about you?
- Now change it up and share what funny thing you would write about your spouse.
- Identify one of these five things that gets in your own way the most (it might be different for each of you): pride, stubbornness, busyness, complacency, and laziness.
- Discuss how you think your personal actions have affected your relationship for better or worse.
- Take turns listing two or three things you used to do for your spouse that you no longer do anymore. Take care in how you respond to one another's statements so there is no shaming or accusing. This is about recognizing our own responsibility in loving and serving our spouse.
- Reminisce about a time in your marriage when you feel your "for better or for worse" vow was tested the most.
  - * What made you stronger during that experience?
  - * What shook your marriage bond during that time?
- Write a living eulogy about your spouse. Grab paper and a pen for each of you and take five or ten minutes to write out what you would say in front of a crowd about your husband or wife. Then, read each of your eulogies aloud together.
  - * If you don't want to write it out, each record a video on your phone and then play them for each other.

Chapter Nineteen

THE AROMA OF HOPE

*O*n a sunny June morning, I walked across the beautiful campus of a Midwest college admiring the trees, flowers, and foliage. There for a writer's conference, I dawdled a little on my way over to the auditorium as I enjoyed the sights, sounds, and smells. There was a pleasant smell I couldn't place. Maybe a mock orange bush in blossom? I didn't see one. I knew it wasn't lilac. Not roses. What was that? Something lightly floral and sweet.

Later, on my way back to the dorm, I smelled it again. Lovely!

But when the scent became stronger and I rounded a corner of a building, I discovered the source of the smell—a blue portable toilet station for the workers who were renovating a section of cobblestone path. Some sort of sanitary drop-in or air freshener inside of that porta-potty gave off what I had assumed came from a flowering plant.

Sometimes, there is a sweet-smelling aroma, even from a toilet, and it makes us stop and take notice. Even in the midst of stinky moments in marriage there are still glimmers of hope, and it's worth stopping to notice them. There are times when I wish there were an easy formula for turning that hope into victory and restoration.

> I would never have thought of using a porta-potty for an example. Would it be okay if I tried out some of my puns here? I think you may have smelled some *toiletrees.*
> Did you just say to me, "Urine a lot of trouble"?
> Man, I'm such a *commodian.*
> –*Phil*

Phil has often said that marriage would be easier if he had an OBD (On-Board Diagnostics) reader for my mind. Let me explain what that is for those who aren't car geeks, myself included. An OBD reader is a hand-held computer that can be plugged into a special port on a car and it reads all of the codes that tell the operator why the check engine light came on.

It solves the mystery for the mechanic because he knows where to begin troubleshooting the problem with the car. Sometimes Phil wishes he knew where to begin troubleshooting when my words or body language indicate a problem, but he has no idea what the problem is.

> This OBD reader for wives would be the best invention ever. If it could be a smartphone app that detects the problem by Bluetooth, that would be so handy. –*Phil*

Sometimes we have no idea what the root problems in a relationship are. There have been many times in our marriage when I'm upset, but I don't know how to explain it. Phil is a fixer, so he wishes there were an easy way to fix every problem. There have also been times when it felt as if the problem was too big, as if we were sliding down a slope toward total breakdown without any sure ideas of how to fix it.

But then a small adjustment brought back the hope that we could survive the challenge and be even better.

Hope Tweaks

If reading this book has been difficult for you because you don't have much hope for your marriage, let's find some. Each tweak is a small tune-up that rekindles hope that we can keep this marriage running for the long haul.

Pray. If you haven't already, commit to praying for your marriage, even if your spouse won't pray with you.

Acknowledge the truth. If your marriage is in a bad place, don't try to pretend like it isn't. The truth is, it hurts. You might feel lonely, rejected, angry, bitter, disappointed, or worthless.

Before you can fix it, it's important to know what is wrong. Is your communication good, but your physical intimacy gone? Do you feel like roommates instead of lovers? Do you have great sex, but can't stand to be in the same room the rest of the time? Was there an affair that you're working to get past? Whatever it is, acknowledge it and then get ready for some hard work.

> God cares about the little details that concern us, not only about what I think of as big stuff. Sometimes, God's voice sounds like this in my head, "Phil, stop being an idiot. Listen to what your wife is saying right now."
>
> I would like it if God's voice sounded more like this, "Phil, you do plenty of stuff with your wife. She's being unreasonable and selfish. She's getting upset over something so petty."
>
> But that's *my* inner voice, and God's sounds a lot more self-sacrificing. It's hard to tell them apart when my own desires shout louder than his. —*Phil*

Don't compare to others. What you see when they're in public may or may not be how their relationship really is—people are great at faking happiness. Focus on your own work to be done and on what's best for you.

Decide you're all in. Be vulnerable enough to risk getting your heart broken in order to remove barriers in your relationship. It's scary, but so is divorce.

Choose to look for hope. When a situation seems hopeless, all we can see are the problems. But when we choose to look for hope, we start to see the good things that are still there. It's sort of like when you research a brand of car and suddenly notice everyone seems to have one. When you look for good things, you start to notice them.

Get advice from the right place. Some of your friends will counsel you to leave your spouse. Some will say that if he or she doesn't meet your needs it's time to move on. Acknowledge that not everyone gives good advice.

> I'm sad for our friends who tried to save their marriages, but who now share custody of children and spend some holidays alone. I'm aware that not every broken marriage can be restored, but if you can try, please give it your all. —*Phil*

I once met for coffee with a woman who wanted to start a business. It was her life-long dream to own a cafe. She even had the location picked out. But her husband wasn't on board with the idea yet. Some of his objections were legitimate, as in financial ones. But there were also other difficulties in their relationship; it wasn't only about the business. Many businesswomen friends advised that if he didn't support her dreams, she should move ahead without him. One of our mutual business contacts advised that she needed to do her life the way she wanted—that her husband had no right to kill her dreams. She posted on social media, and the advice there was similar.

But she decided to wait on it for a little longer. I'm so proud of her for waiting. It was fewer than five years later when she and her husband had the finances to move forward with her dream. It's the most darling place—and he even helps at the restaurant! Their marriage is a work in progress, but she almost gave it up.

Be ready to forgive. We talked a lot about this in chapter 15. This might be a huge step if forgiving involves getting past an affair. It might be easier in other situations, such as when forgiving each other for growing apathetic. Prepare your heart to forgive your spouse for what they have done to cause pain for you. This is a choice that comes with a challenge— one that asks you to be humble and gracious. It means setting aside blame and becoming a team again.

Believe in miracles. Miracles are not only for other couples. First, ask God to work a miracle in you. We can't change another person, but we can change us. After God has worked a miracle in your own heart, then you are ready to pray for a miracle in your marriage.

Whenever I have fixated on fixing Phil (there's a tongue twister for you) I put all the blame on him for why a transformation hasn't happened yet in a conflict between us. I've learned to invite God into my own thoughts and attitudes and ask him to do some housekeeping there. It does so much for my perspective about the things that make me fume.

There are a lot of questions that come while we're holding out for a miracle. What if my spouse never changes? What if I'm doomed to an unhappy life? What if this is as good as it gets?

What if we changed those "what if" questions to focus on the other person, instead of me, me, me? For example:

> If I could answer the question of why some couples can work it out and others struggle until they sign divorce papers, I'd probably have a nice little counseling practice somewhere instead of shed full of Jeep parts and project vehicles. I won't meet most of the people who read this book, but I am praying that each of you would hold on to hope for your marriage. I also pray that each of you would be willing to do your part in restoring your marriage. —*Phil*

- What if I let go of my expectations?
- What if I broke the ice?
- What if I love him or her just as they are?
- What if I showed grace?
- What if I lived for God's approval instead of people's approval?
- What if I released bitterness, pride, and anger?

How to Pray for Hope

Prayer is effective because it helps us to align our human and faulty thinking with the perfection of our holy God. It has more effect on us than it does on him. But how do you pray when your marriage is about to break? We don't want to pretend here that despite the best efforts, sometimes a spouse walks away, files for divorce, and you're left holding the pieces. But we want to hope that a miracle comes before it comes to that. Here are some prayers for your marriage—whether it's at the breaking point, or on the right track:

- **God, equip me.** Ask God to give you his love for your spouse. Ask for patience, endurance, humility, and peace.

- **God, heal me.** Ask him to soothe the wounds that have come from rejection, harsh words, and apathy. Pray for emotional healing and restoration.
- **God, make me courageous.** Ask God to make you brave as you take a risk for the sake of restoring your marriage. Pray for boldness in speaking your heart calmly and without blame.
- **God, prepare me.** Pray that God would prepare you for whatever challenges are ahead. He might prepare you by bringing a mentor to walk you through it or by leading you to a resource you can read. He might show you verses in his Word to prepare you.
- **God, lead me.** Ask for wisdom to know if an idea is from him or from yourself. Pray for wisdom in sorting through the input from other people and outside sources.
- **God, give me grace.** Pray for willingness to forgive and overlook offenses. Ask for the will to let go of grudges, even if you were in the right.
- **God, teach me.** As you get into God's Word and study, ask him to specifically show you what he wants to teach you that will help your marriage.
- **God, change me.** Pray for God's help in applying what he teaches you, that you would be focused on changing you, and not on changing your spouse.

When I think of how I used to pray, I remember my prayers being more about changing other people. Whether it was in my marriage or about people at work, I preferred to think that others needed fixing more than me. Now I pray more: God change me and bless them. —*Phil*

You've probably heard others talk about their spouse as their better half. In chapter 16, we talked about a covenant marriage and how we're not halves that complete each other. We are whole. This is because Christ completes us, not our spouse. We complement each other, but we do not complete each other. If you're waiting and praying for restoration in your marriage, you are not half of a person. In Jesus, you are complete. Fall in love with Jesus. Practice expressing the kind of love Jesus has—that gives all and expects nothing in return—and let God handle the results.

The greatest commandments require self-sacrifice. The first commandment Jesus gave is to love God with all our heart, soul, mind, and strength. The second one is to love others as we love ourselves (see Matthew 22:36–40). Love God, love people. He didn't say either would be easy—there are days when I am not an easy person to love! I tend to put my wants and desires above Phil's way too often.

Jesus lived by example, and I'm thankful that he showed what it was like to love even when the very people for whom he gave up everything rejected and mocked him. He was misunderstood, but he surrendered to the will of God his Father. And he gave it all for us. So, whether or not our spouse reciprocates, God asks us to show love through our words and actions.

As you work toward a marriage that produces joy, remember these things:

God created you.

God loves you.

God knows you.

God has not abandoned you.

Tune-Up Time

- Warm up with a little fun: What is a scent or odor most people can't stand that you actually like?
- Describe a memory of a season in your relationship where you weren't sure if you were going to make it as a couple (maybe you're in one now). What was it that gave you enough hope to keep trying?
- Practice getting to the truth. Grab a notecard, a scrap of paper, or a napkin for each of you. Take a minute to think about what you need to acknowledge in your relationship that you've tried to pretend isn't a problem. Write one short statement that describes what it is.
  - * Now take turns reading what you wrote.
  - * Discuss a next step for how you're going to work on that issue together.
- There is no computer that can interpret what your spouse is feeling when he or she is upset. Discuss ways you can each support one another without trying to fix each other. List specific actions or words that help each of you to feel understood and validated when you're upset.
- Discuss ways you could both rely on God's Word more individually and as a couple. Make a plan for how you are going to read and discuss the Bible on a more regular basis together. When will you do it? Where? How?

Chapter Twenty

HAPPILY EVER AFTER

This book began with once upon a time, so it is only appropriate that it should end with happily ever after, right? Not so fast.

The purpose for marriage is not to make us happy. I sincerely hope you are happily married, but that isn't the purpose for marriage. Remember the passage from Ephesians I shared in chapter 16? That was a picture of Jesus Christ sacrificing his life for the sake of his followers, and as the church, we become the bride of Christ. He gave his life on the cross in an agonizing crucifixion. That doesn't sound like happily ever after.

Please. I'm not saying your marriage should feel like an agonizing crucifixion. Oh my, no. But back when you were single, did you long for the happiness that marriage would bring? Did it feel as if you couldn't possibly find happily ever after without a companion? One by one your friends married off, and you wanted that too.

Then you got married. And you discovered it was hard work to love someone unconditionally. It was hard work to put their needs above yours. Human beings get crabby and say things they don't mean. It felt awful

> When Michelle went off to college, I decided that four years away was going to be a long time. So, on the first weekend when I went to visit, I had planned to break things off. But then I tried to show off by doing a hurdle over a chain roadblock and sprained my ankle. I lost the nerve to follow through when she was icing my foot and taking care of me. I decided she was worth waiting for. —*Phil*

when your feelings were hurt and you faced rejection from the man or woman of your dreams. Remember your first argument? How did that feel?

When Conflict Comes

We had some little disagreements before our wedding, but I don't recall any big fights. If we did have disagreements, it felt as if we could get past anything. We were in love after all.

Our first big conflict happened several months into our marriage and a few hours before Phil's cousin's wedding. I remember it because it felt so anti-utopian to be so mad at him right before Shawn and Susan said their vows.

We had traveled from Wisconsin to Michigan, and we were staying in a pop-up camper that was set up inside Phil's uncle and aunt's garage. When it came time to start getting ready for the wedding, I went to look for the hanging zipper bag that contained my dress. I couldn't find it. At this point it became sort of like a Dr. Seuss book but with more of a desperate and humorless flair. It was not in the house. It was not in the truck. It was not in the car, nor was it near or far. It was not here or there. It was not anywhere.

"Phil, have you seen my hanging bag?"

"No. What did it look like?"

"Black. It has a zipper." Nondescriptive, but all I had. "It was hanging on our closet door with yours when we packed."

"Mine is here."

"Yes, I see that. But you carried

> Look here and there and near and far, and you won't find them in the car. You're on the right track, you have quite a knack, now that you know I don't know how to pack. —*Phil*

our bags out to the truck and my hanging bag was situated in front of yours on the door."

This is where the conversation started to escalate as I had the realization that in order for his bag to have arrived in Michigan for the wedding, it meant he would have had to lift mine off the hook, grab his from behind, and put mine back on the hook. I started to get that blurry feeling I get right before I say something I regret. We had words. I don't remember what they were. Well, I had words. He was kind of speechless.

I can honestly say I have never reconciled the idea that someone could logically not notice that this bag also needed to go in the car. Of course, I've long since forgiven him, but in that moment, I wanted to have an all-out, on-the-floor temper tantrum. But we had no time. We had to figure out what to do. I had nylon stockings and a slip, and that wasn't going to be appropriate attire for a wedding.

My shoes were with the dress, so I didn't have those either. And I was not the same size as any of the other guests in the household that weekend. Nor did I feel like wearing something borrowed from Aunt Shirley. No offense to her style. I was twenty and she was in her 50s. (Which mysteriously no longer sounds "old" now that I'm past fifty!)

We drove as fast as we could to the closest Meijer store, which is sort of like a Target or a Super Walmart. They have groceries, garden stuff, clothing, and shoes.

We didn't have much time, so I had to choose quickly, which is not something I'm known for. I like to browse the clearance racks and find the perfect thing. I needed to find a dress that worked, not the cheapest one.

We spent fifty dollars on that dress, which was more than I had ever spent on an item of clothing before, except for my wedding gown, which was one hundred dollars. We purchased the cheapest pair of black pumps to go with it and were on our way.

We made it to the wedding in time and we made up. But if you had asked us right then, neither of us was happy.

If you don't have some moments of conflict in a relationship, I have to

> I bought you some shoes and I purchased a dress, and by hook or by crook I got out of that mess.
> —*Phil*

wonder if you're really human. Passion goes both ways, both positive and negative. If we have enough passion to love, then we will have enough passion to fight. It's what we do with that passion that makes or breaks us.

> What?! My charm isn't enough for you to have happily ever after? Not even the emojis I text to you? *–Phil*

We have not always been happy in our marriage. Phil has not always met my needs. He has not always fulfilled my wishes or my dreams. I haven't always fulfilled his either. But we stuck it out because we know that happiness is not the main purpose of our marriage.

The problem with thinking marriage is made to make you happy is that if you aren't happy, you start to think you found the wrong person. And if you think you found the wrong person, your eye starts to wander. You don't voice it aloud, but you might think, "This gal at my office really gets me. She makes me smile. And I haven't smiled in a long time at home." Or, "This guy I see at the gym has noticed my curves. I've lost forty pounds and my husband acts as if I'm no more attractive than his best buddy. What's up with that?"

Chasing After Happy

When our brains start to head in the direction of seeking happiness or physical and emotional needs, we say things that push our spouses even further away. For example, a situation that goes something like this:

It's a Saturday morning, and your husband snuggles over to your side of the bed. "I have an idea for how we could start the weekend," he says.

You try to make a barrier by tucking the sheets under your body and then rolling back onto them. This restrains his attempts at seeking parts of your body. "I'm not in the mood."

He sighs and does a Jekyll and Hyde move. The sweet amorous husband is now ready for attack. "Do you know how many women at the office would be happy to have me?"

Jab.

Silence.

"I'm just kidding. It isn't like I would cheat on you or anything. But no one would fault me for it."

This is one of those moments where a "joke" isn't funny, and words hurt. It would be crazy to put all of the blame on the husband here. But let's step out of the action and do a picture-in-picture of this moment.

He's trying to say that when she rejects him, he feels undesirable. But he also doesn't know what's going on inside of her head. Where libido is lacking, shame is abundant. When he implies that there are a lot of other women who would be happy to do what she is not willing to do in this moment, it piles on more shame. She hasn't yet figured out what to do when her brain and her body won't align. Again, neither is happy.

> That's a lot of hostility for one Saturday morning. This isn't going to end well. *—Phil*

Let's not put all of the blame for the lack of libido on her either. If you're a jerk for 90 percent of the day, but nice when you hope your wife might jump your bones, think again. Wife, if you nag and criticize and put down all day long, and then you wonder why he treats you like an object to only meet his physical needs, consider if you might be too prickly.

This is a multilayered picture with a lot of emotions flying around. If happiness is your only focus and neither person is happy, then each starts to wonder if there is a different way to be happy. Both might believe they deserve to be happy.

❧

Let's imagine that they try to discuss this but while still focused on their own needs. That conversation might go down something like this:

"I want to be in the mood. I don't know what's wrong with me. Maybe I'm tired. Maybe it's hormones. If only you would do more to help me, I might have more energy to meet your needs."

Whoa, she dumped that over to him for blame.

"At least I'm not down at the bar every night getting drunk with my buddies and dancing with the girls."

Oh, he went there and used the "at least" argument. He wants her to believe she's making a huge deal and that he isn't "that bad," another expression I don't love.

> I've never tried using "at least" or "not that bad." Okay. True story: I have tried it, and Michelle didn't like it. And saying there are other women out there who would be happy to have me could potentially lead to me standing on the front steps with a suitcase. *—Phil*

"We never talk anymore. You're always watching TV."

See that? She went for never and always, which she knows aren't true, but it makes a better argument.

"That's because I want to stay out of your way when you're in a bad mood."

If you've had a discussion similar to this one, you know it never ends well. They probably move on with their weekend, and she might hang out with her friends and complain about how her husband doesn't meet her emotional needs anymore and how she isn't happy. He might go out to the bar with his friends in a moment of rebellion and tell them that his wife isn't doing her duty.

Sacred Marriage

Marriage is called holy matrimony sometimes. Being holy means being set apart. What if marriage wasn't designed to make us happy, but to make us holy? What if it was to teach us how to be set apart to God and then living to please him? Gary Thomas has referred to this as a sacred marriage in his book, where he talks about how marriage can help us deepen our relationship with God.[12]

If all we ever pursue is our own happiness, life will be fun for a while, but not forever. Eventually, we'll walk all over enough people that we have no more friends. We will lose the respect of coworkers, make dumb decisions about finances, and become downright annoying to people.

There was a guy like that in a parable Jesus told. It's in Luke 15. This son wanted to be happy, so he asked his dad for his inheritance because he wanted it before his dad died, and he didn't want to wait. He left home and made a big mess of his life while he wasted all of the money and partied it up. Then, when he was at his lowest, he went crawling back to his dad and begged for forgiveness.

If you have been living for happiness in your marriage, maybe it's time to come back to each other and pursue holiness together. You might just discover that if you pursue holiness first, happiness will trail right along behind.

> I like my comfort zone, but I realize that for God to make us into who he wants us to be, there will be some discomfort involved—even sharing very personal stories with readers and making our children uncomfortable.
>
> If our discomfort leads to helping someone else, then I hope it also leads to helping them discover the kind of life that Jesus came to bring.
>
> I'm still practicing at pursuing holiness above my personal happiness. That also makes me a better husband. Not perfect. Better. —*Phil*

Ever After

We couldn't have written this book five years ago. We're always a work in progress, but right then, there were some big things that we still hadn't tackled. We are working on them and have made much progress. I couldn't have written this book then because I wasn't ready to be vulnerable. I would have left out the hard chapters to write.

We don't have all of the answers. Mostly, I want our story to help someone else hang on for dear life when they consider letting go. I want to be the cheerleader who says, "You can do it with God's help."

I've seen marriages survive affairs. I don't know how, except for God. I've seen friends discover a deep connection in the fall and winter of their marriage that wasn't there in the spring or summer decades. Again, it was God. Laughter is alive and well in our household, and I enjoy spending time with my husband. That is truly a testimony to God's power.

I also celebrate the couples who we knew in high school who have made it to thirty years and beyond. Like signing yearbooks, it feels like we should all write nice messages on one another's photos: "You are an amazing couple! I hope you have a great second half of life. Stay cool and rock on."

If you want to pursue holiness over happiness in your marriage, self-reflection is helpful. Here are some questions to ask:

- How is God shaping my character as he teaches me to love my spouse?
- How has marriage been a petri dish that points out places where I need to grow in the character of Christ?
- How can I serve, rather than be served?
- How can I learn to listen before acting, to be gentle instead of shouting, to speak kindly instead of harshly, or to be less critical when my spouse disappoints me?
- How has God uniquely paired me with my spouse in ways that soften my edges or complement my strengths?
- What does God want to do through our story that will bring him glory?

Thank you for caring enough to let our journey and our story inspire something in your own marriage to make it a classic. As your odometer climbs, we hope the ending of your long love story is, "And they all lived holy ever after."

> As God leads you outside of your comfort zone, I hope you enjoy the adventure. There might be a breakdown or a flat tire along the way, but it's all part of the journey. Keep your marriage tuned up, and when you hear something "clunking" pay attention. Ignorance is not bliss. I pray yours is a long and classic marriage. —*Phil*

Tune-Up Time

- When you were single, what made you want to be married?
  * How has being married fulfilled this desire?
  * How has it not fulfilled this desire?
- What has marriage revealed about your own rough edges that needed some work? What was surprising about this for you?
- Name one weakness (your own) that has been exposed during the course of your marriage. Listen to each other without critique as you share your own weakness. What will you do in the next two weeks to begin work on this weakness? Declare it out loud to your spouse as your commitment.
- Discuss the idea of how marriage can make you more like God. How does this contrast with the idea of expecting your marriage to make you happy?
- Talk about what you think of the idea of pursuing God more and letting happiness trail after that as a benefit rather than a goal.
- Take a few minutes to each write out a paragraph or two about where you see your marriage in the next five to ten years. Write it as if you already are that couple.
  * Now share what you wrote with one another, and together identify three priorities you'll pursue as action steps as a result of reading this book.

Resources

You'll find downloadable versions of the discussion questions from each chapter of this book, plus a curated list of other helpful tools and resources for marriage and relationships, at **classicmarriagebook.com**.

This list includes:

- Marriage books
- Video series for couples
- Couples retreats and getaways
- Date night resources
- Discussion questions
- And more!

About the Authors

*M*ichelle Rayburn *is the author* of five books, including *The Repurposed and Upcycled Life: When God Turns Trash to Treasure*. She has a Master of Arts in ministry leadership with an emphasis on pastoral counseling. She has published Bible studies, articles, and devotionals in places such as *Focus on the Family, Christian Communicator, Chicken Soup for the Soul, Vista, Today's Christian Living*, and more. She has also written for ChristianBibleStudies.com.

She hosts a weekly podcast called *Life, Repurposed* and loves to help people discover ways to find joy in the midst of the trashy stuff of life. Michelle enjoys transforming flea market finds into treasures for their home; this mostly involves dragging Phil into projects that require his muscle and skill.

Speaking of Phil Rayburn, he has been entertaining people with his dry sense of humor around dinner tables and in living rooms for over fifty years—but never from stage or in print. He is the director of maintenance at a Christian camp, and spends his days plowing snow, mowing lawns, chopping firewood, fixing tractors, and unclogging toilets. He enjoys an annual trip or two to the Minnesota Boundary Waters Canoe Area, where he and the boys are off the grid for a week at a time to fish, canoe, and do guy stuff that grosses out Michelle. He also can be found regularly with his head under the hood of a classic Jeep or an old truck of any sort. His idea of a weekend project involves replacing an engine in a vehicle, and he almost always smells of motor oil, gasoline, or wood smoke from the heater in the shop.

Michelle and Phil have been married for thirty years and have two adult sons and two daughters-in-love. Together they enjoy hiking, road trips, and reality TV shows. They live in northern Wisconsin in a one-hundred-year-old former church.

Connect with Michelle:

Facebook: @michelle.rayburn.author
Instagram: @michellerayburn
Twitter: @michellerayburn

Learn more and find other books at **www.michellerayburn.com**.

The Repurposed and Upcycled Life: When God Turns Trash To Treasure
(Book and women's small group Bible study workbook)

Thank You Notes

Thank you, readers, for trusting us with your time. If you didn't laugh or improve your marriage, we did something wrong and we will try again. Maybe in another thirty years.

Thank you, sons, for still speaking to us after we got real and ventured into TMI, for marrying well, and loving Jesus.

Thank you, daughters-in-law, for taking our last name and forgiving us for whatever quirks we couldn't fix before we launched our boys into the world.

Thank you, our wonderful parents, for the example of staying married for better or for worse and all that other stuff.

Thank you, mistakes, for giving us enough material to write seventy thousand words about how we still made it past thirty years.

Thank you, Jesus, for covering all those mistakes with the power of your grace.

Thank you, dishes and housework, for providing the perfect scenario to test our degree of self-sacrifice.

Thank you, sleep deprivation and hunger, for making our character flaws painfully obvious.

Thank you, marriage experts, for doing a much better job of sounding smart with the advice you give. You make it look easy.

Thank you, rusty Jeeps, for being the inspiration for this book. You are the wind beneath our wings. When you start, that is.

Thank you, pizza, for being the easiest meal two empty nesters could put together when date night is here and we forgot to plan something nutritious.

Thank you, God, for proving you had a plan and purpose for our marriage that we were too immature to see until we had been together for more than a quarter century.

Endnotes

1   Doug Stone, vocalist, "Little Houses," by Victor Jara, track 1 on *Greatest Hits, Vol. 1*, Epic Records,1994.

2   Gretchen Livingston, "Childlessness," Pew Research Center, May 7, 2015, https://www.pewsocialtrends.org/2015/05/07/childlessness/.

3   "Love language" is a term coined by Dr. Gary Chapman, author of *The Five Love Languages*, https://www.5lovelanguages.com/.

4   Gary Chapman, *The Five Love Languages: How to Express Heartfelt Commitment to Your Mate* (Northfield Publishing, 1992, updated in 2015).

5   Gil Greengross Ph.D., "How Humor Can Change Your Relationship," *Psychology Today*, November 17, 2018, https://www.psychologytoday.com/us/blog/humor-sapiens/201811/how-humor-can-change-your-relationship/.

6   "eharmony Puts Humor to the Test: Can Laughter Predict Love," Cison PR Newswire, September 20, 2017, accessed 5/20/2019, https://www.prnewswire.com/news-releases/eharmony-puts-humor-to-the-test-can-laughter-predict-love-300522493.html/.

7   *Wordreference.com*, s.v. "Keel," accessed June 25, 2020, https://www.wordreference.com/definition/keel/.

8   "PFFT! You Was Gone!" is attributed to Bix Reichner, who purchased the copyright for the song in 1958 from Bob Newman (alias Lee Roberts), https://www.zeroto180.org/?p=23560/.

9   "H1586 - Gomer - Strong's Hebrew Lexicon (NLT)." Blue Letter Bible. Accessed March 22, 2020, https://www.blueletterbible.org//lang/lexicon/lexicon.cfm?Strongs=h1586&t=NLT/.

10 Richard L Strauss, "Undying Love—The Story of Hosea and Gomer," Bible.org, published June 28, 2004, accessed March 22, 2020, https://bible.org/seriespage/8-undying-love-story-hosea-and-gomer/.

11 *NIV Study Bible* (Grand Rapids: Zondervan, 2011) footnote on 1 Peter 1:16.

12 Gary Thomas, *Sacred Marriage* (Grand Rapids: Zondervan, 2000).

13 *The Princess Bride*, directed by Rob Reiner (20th Century Fox, 1987).

Made in the USA
Middletown, DE
03 October 2022